Transport Today

Series Editor: Cara Acred

Volume 278

Independence Educational Publishers

First published by Independence Educational Publishers

The Studio, High Green

Great Shelford

Cambridge CB22 5EG

England

© Independence 2015

Photocopy licence

The material in this book is protected by copyright. However, the

purchaser is free to make multiple copies of particular articles for instructional

purposes for immediate use within the purchasing institution.

Making copies of the entire book is not permitted.

British Library Cataloguing in Publication Data

Transport today. -- (Issues ; 278)

1. Transportation. 2. Transportation--Environmental

aspects. 3. Transportation and state.

I. Series II. Acred, Cara editor.

388-dc23

ISBN-13: 9781861687067

Printed in Great Britain

Zenith Print Group

Contents

Introduction

Transport Today is Volume 278 in the **ISSUES** series. The aim of the series is to offer current, diverse information about important issues in our world, from a UK perspective.

ABOUT TRANSPORT TODAY

With travel trends constantly evolving, we are surrounded by debates about the future of transport, both globally and in the UK. This book explores the relationship between transport and the environment, considering the health implications of our commute to work and whether car sharing encourages green habits on and off the road. It also looks at current and future issues such as transport poverty, road safety, electric vehicles and driverless cars.

OUR SOURCES

Titles in the **ISSUES** series are designed to function as educational resource books, providing a balanced overview of a specific subject.

The information in our books is comprised of facts, articles and opinions from many different sources, including:

⇨ Newspaper reports and opinion pieces

⇨ Website factsheets

⇨ Magazine and journal articles

⇨ Statistics and surveys

⇨ Government reports

⇨ Literature from special interest groups

A NOTE ON CRITICAL EVALUATION

Because the information reprinted here is from a number of different sources, readers should bear in mind the origin of the text and whether the source is likely to have a particular bias when presenting information (or when conducting their research). It is hoped that, as you read about the many aspects of the issues explored in this book, you will critically evaluate the information presented.

It is important that you decide whether you are being presented with facts or opinions. Does the writer give a biased or unbiased report? If an opinion is being expressed, do you agree with the writer? Is there potential bias to the 'facts' or statistics behind an article?

ASSIGNMENTS

In the back of this book, you will find a selection of assignments designed to help you engage with the articles you have been reading and to explore your own opinions. Some tasks will take longer than others and there is a mixture of design, writing and research-based activities that you can complete alone or in a group.

FURTHER RESEARCH

At the end of each article we have listed its source and a website that you can visit if you would like to conduct your own research. Please remember to critically evaluate any sources that you consult and consider whether the information you are viewing is accurate and unbiased.

Useful weblinks

www.20splentyforus.org.uk

www.ashfordfor.com

www.bettertransport.org.uk

www.cam.ac.uk

www.cedar.org.uk

www.climateandus.com

www.disabilitynewsservice.com

www.euractiv.com

www.hs2actionalliance.org

www.marshalls.com

www.racfoundation.org

www.rtcc.org

www.securingthefuture.co.uk

www.sustrans.org.uk

www.theiet.org

www.who.int

National Travel Survey: England 2013

Trends since the early 1970s.

The average distance people travel per year has increased by 47%. Most of this growth occurred during the 1970s and 1980s and was largely due to an increase in average trip lengths, which have risen by 52% since the early 1970s.

Trip rates increased until the mid-1990s, but have since fallen and are below the 1970s' level. However, trips of over one mile have increased by 27% since the early 1970s. Since the late 1990s, the average distance travelled and average trip lengths have generally levelled off.

Trends since 1995/97

Between 1995/97 and 2013 there was a steady falling trend in trip rates. In 2013, on average each person made 923 trips per year, compared with 1,094 in 1995/97 – a fall of 16% and the lowest trip rate recorded. For trips over one mile in length, there was a fall of only 6%.

The average distance travelled per person per year was 6% lower in 2013 than in 1995/97 – 6,983 miles compared with 6,584 miles. Distance travelled peaked in 2003 at 7,202 miles.

The average trip length increased by 12% from 6.4 miles in 1995/97 to 7.1 miles in 2013.

Time spent travelling has remained fairly static over time at around an hour a day. In 2013, residents of England spent an average of 364 hours per year travelling compared to 372 hours in 1995/97. Average trip time has increased by 16% over the period, from 20.4 minutes to 23.7 minutes.

Of all trips made in 2013, 18% were less than one mile in length, 67% less than five miles and 95% were less than 25 miles.

How we travel

This section presents statistics on the use of different transport modes in 2013 by residents of England and changes over time.

64% of all trips were made by car (as a driver or passenger) in 2013. Walking trips accounted for 22% of all trips. Therefore, two transports modes – car and walking – accounted for 86% of all trips in 2013.

Car travel again forms the largest proportion when mode share is presented in terms of distance travelled. In 2013, 77% of total distance travelled was by car.

Buses (both local and non-local) accounted for a greater proportion of all trips than rail (both surface rail and London Underground) at 7% and 3%, respectively. However, as local bus trips on average are shorter in length, bus trips overall accounted for only 5% of total distance travelled whereas rail accounted for 10%.

The largest downward contributions to the overall decrease in trip rates recorded between 1995/97 and 2013 have come from two transport modes: walking and car (as a driver or passenger).

The average number of trips per person per year broadly increases with age up to 40–49 years and then decreases among older age groups. Overall, women make more trips than men in a year on average, but men travel further.

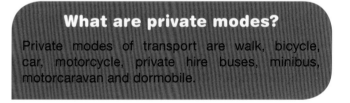

What are private modes?

Private modes of transport are walk, bicycle, car, motorcycle, private hire buses, minibus, motorcaravan and dormobile.

Private modes of transport

In 2013, 89% of all trips were by private transport modes. Trips by private transport modes have decreased by 18% since 1995/97.

Presenting the trip rate as indices means that the change in the number of walking trips since 1995/97 can be compared with the change in other private transport modes such as car travel (as a driver or passenger).

What is a trip?

The basic unit of travel in the National Travel Survey is a trip, defined as a one-way course of travel with a single main purpose.

What are trip rates?

Trip rates are the 'average' number of trips per person per year, and are calculated based on whether a person makes that type of trip or not.

Walking and car trips

Walking trips in particular have fallen significantly over time from 292 trips per person per year in 1995/97 to 203 trips in 2013, a 30% decrease. The 2013 walking trip rate was the lowest over this period and when asked, 20% of respondents said that they walk for 20 minutes or more less than once a year or never.

Of all trips less than one mile in length 78% were walking trips.

Between 1995/97 and 2013 the average number of car driver trips and passenger trips both decreased by 12%. Across the same period, the average distance travelled by car driver also decreased by 12% from 3,660 miles per person per year to 3,235 miles. In terms of time spent travelling, each person, on average, spent 212 hours travelling by car (as a driver or passenger) in 2013 compared with 225 hours in 1995/97.

Changes in car usage tend to be affected by wider economic factors, such as the state of the economy and fuel prices, which influence car ownership and the trip behaviour of car users. Increases to the cost of motoring could also be expected to have a negative effect on car use.

These factors are all likely to have affected car use since 1995/97. Although the NTS has shown a 12% decrease in car driver distance travelled per person over this period, accounting for population growth in England would illustrate a smaller decline in total distance travelled by car.

The NTS can be used to show car use by gender and a divergent trend in car use can be seen for men and women. Men drive around twice as many miles per year, on average, as women (4,209 miles compared with 2,291 miles). However, since 1995/97 the average number of car driver trips by men has fallen by 23% and average distance travelled by 22%. This compares to a 4% increase in car driver trips and a 15% increase in distance travelled by women. The trend in car usage by men and women are closely related to the differences in licence holding.

Bicycle trips

Counting bicycle stages rather than trips allows us to include journeys that involve a bicycle but where this is not the main form of transport (for example, cycling to a railway station to then catch the train).

In 2013, 1% of all stages were made by bicycle. Between 1995/97 and 2013 the average number of bicycle stages per person per year has fallen from 20 stages in 1995/97 to 15 stages in 2013; a fall of 25%.

However, due to the relatively small number of cyclists in the NTS sample there is annual volatility in the cycling data and bicycle stages as a proportion of all stages generally fluctuates between 1% and 2%. Looking at cycling activity in terms of average distance travelled tells a different story when compared with the decline in the average number of cycling stages.

Average distance travelled by bicycle increased by 8% from 46 miles per person per year in 1995/97 to 49 miles in 2013. The average distance travelled by bicycle by London residents has increased by 55% since 1995/97.

Public modes of transport

Public transport's share of all trips has increased slightly from 9% in 1995/97 to 11% in 2013. In 1995/97, on average, each person made 100 public transport trips per year compared with 106 public transport trips in 2013, an increase of 6%.

The largest upward contributions to the increase in public transport's share of all trips has come from London buses and surface rail. The average number of London bus trips and surface rail trips has increased by 45% and 67%, respectively, between 1995/97 and 2013. Other local bus (buses outside of London) trips have decreased by 18%.

In 2003, 52% of respondents said that they use surface rail less than

What are public modes?

Public modes of transport are local bus in London, other local bus, surface rail, London Underground, light rail taxi, domestic air and ferry.

once a year, or never. In 2013 this had fallen to 41%.

In terms of average distance travelled, London bus has increased by 68%, surface rail by 66% and other local bus has shown a small decline of 1%.

The NTS shows that bus use, as a proportion of all trips, was highest among those aged 17–20, accounting for 18% of all trips in this age group.

The next highest proportion was for those aged 60+, reflecting the availability of concessionary travel schemes for older passengers. In 2013, 76% of eligible older people in England had a concessionary pass (79% of women and 73% of men). The region with the highest take-up rate is London with 87% of eligible residents holding a concessionary pass. Overall, there is considerable variation between take-up rates in urban and rural areas with 57% take-up in the most rural areas (rural villages, hamlets and isolated dwellings) compared with 83% in urban conurbations.

How a person's mobility influences how they travel

Overall, 11% of adults reported having a mobility difficulty in 2013 (adults, those aged 16+, who say they have difficulties travelling on foot, by bus or both are classified as having mobility difficulties). The proportion of adults with mobility difficulties increases greatly with age. 31% of individuals aged 70+ had problems walking or using a bus, compared with 3% of those aged 16–49. This increase with age is more marked among women than men, although the proportion of women 70+ with mobility problems may be increased by the higher number of women living to very old age.

Those reporting mobility difficulties make fewer trips, on average, across all age groups. This is largely due to fewer trips as a car driver or by walking. People with mobility difficulties also make fewer commuting, education or leisure trips on average, partly reflecting the age profile.

Why people travel

In 2013, the most common trip purpose was shopping, which accounted for 20% of all trips, followed by personal business and other escort trips with 19% of all trips. The least common trip purposes were for education (12% of all trips) and business (3% of all trips).

In 2013, the trip purpose with the highest share of distance travelled was other leisure with 21% of all trips – this purpose mostly consisted of travel for entertainment purposes, sport, holidays and day trips. A further 20% of distance travelled was to visit friends. 19% of all distance travelled was for commuting purposes, whilst education trips only represented 5% of all distance travelled.

Trip length by purpose

Average trip distances have been increasing since 1995/97.

The most common purpose for a long distance trip (those of over 50 miles) was to visit friends at their home, accounting for 22% of all trips over 50 miles. As long distance trips increase in distance they are more

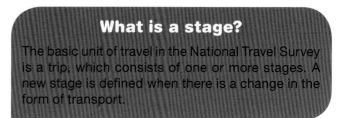

What is a stage?

The basic unit of travel in the National Travel Survey is a trip, which consists of one or more stages. A new stage is defined when there is a change in the form of transport.

likely to be for business or holiday purposes. In 2013, 16% and 8% of trips between 50 and 75 miles were for business or holiday purposes, respectively. These proportions increase to 21% and 45% for trips 350 miles and over.

⇨ The above information is reprinted with kind permission from the Department for Transport. Please visit www. gov.uk/transport for further information.

Keeping the nation moving

Facts on fuels, cars and drivers.

Introduction

To all intents and purposes cars are public transport: they carry most members of the public, most of the time. 90% of all passenger miles travelled in Great Britain are on the roads. Just 9% are on the railways and around 1% in the air. The vast majority of road mileage is completed by car, van or taxi – 83% of the overall total. That's why almost all of Britain's 35.8 million drivers are concerned about the cost of filling up. What follows is intended to help shine a light on both fuel prices and the nation's reliance on car travel.

Source: DfT Transport Statistics GB

Breakdown of the pump price

As of 2 July 2014 the petrol price was 131.6p a litre (diesel was 136.3p).

Of this:

⇨ 21.94p of the total price is VAT (16.7%)

⇨ 57.95p of the total price is fuel duty (44.0%)

⇨ 51.73p of the total price covers the costs of oil, fuel production and supply, and profit margin (39.3%)

Therefore, 60.7% of the pump price of petrol goes to the Chancellor.

The rate of duty was last changed in March 2011 when it was reduced by 1p to 57.95p. The duty rate is the same for both petrol and diesel. The rate of duty last went up on 1 January 2011; from 58.19p to 58.95p.

Source: DECC, RAC Foundation

Fuel price highs

Petrol hit a record high of 142.17p a litre on 16 April 2012.

Diesel hit a record high of 148.04p a litre on the same day.

Source: DECC

UK vs EU fuel prices

As of 2 July 2014 the UK had the eighth highest petrol price in the 28-member EU. The Netherlands, Italy, Denmark, Belgium, Portugal, Germany and Greece all had higher pump prices. As of the same date the UK had the highest diesel price in Europe.

Source: Europe's Energy Portal, RAC Foundation

Oil price

On 2 July 2014 a barrel of Brent crude oil cost $111.00.

On 28 August 2013 a barrel of Brent crude oil hit a 12-month high of $117.34.

On 11 July 2008 a barrel of Brent crude oil hit an all-time whigh of $148.

Source: Financial Times

Number of drivers

There are 35.8 million licensed drivers in Great Britain (73% of all people aged 17 or over) up from 31.4 million in 2000.

There are 19.2 million male drivers and 16.7 million female drivers.

Source: DfT

National Travel Survey NTS0201

Number of registered vehicles

There are 35.2 million licensed vehicles in Great Britain including:

⇨ 29.3 million cars (of which 9,412 are electric)

⇨ 3.4 million vans

⇨ 465,860 lorries

Source: DfT Statistics VEH0103, VEH0130

Vehicles per household

31% of households have two or more cars or vans.

44% of households have one car or van.

25% of households have no car or van.

Source: DfT National Travel Survey NTS0205

Low-income households

In those households in the lowest income quintile (fifth) 48% have no car.

Each person in households in the lowest income quintile makes an average of 400 trips per year by car as a driver or passenger compared with 15 trips by rail and Tube.

On average each person in these households travels 2,706 miles by car compared to 318 miles by rail and Tube.

Source: DfT National Travel Survey NTS0703, NTS0705

Number of journeys by car

Of all the trips made in Great Britain:

⇨ 64% are as a car driver or passenger (main mode)

⇨ 22% are on foot

⇨ 6% are by bus

⇨ 3% are by rail and Tube

78% of distance travelled by all modes, including walking, is as a car driver or passenger.

Source: DfT National Travel Survey NTS0301, NTS0302

Average vehicle mileage

The average petrol car travels 6,900 miles per year.

The average diesel car travels 11,200 miles per year.

On average, a car covers 2,600 miles a year on commuter journeys and 900 miles on business.

Source: DfT National Travel Survey NTS0901, NTS0902

Journey purpose

Of those journeys where a car or a van is the main mode of travel:

⇨ 29% are for leisure

⇨ 20% are for business or commuting

⇨ 20% are for shopping

⇨ 12% are driving someone else

⇨ 10% are on personal business

⇨ 9% are for taking children to school or accessing education

Note: Due to rounding the percentages above may not add up to 100%.

67% of commuting/business trips are by car (as main mode). By comparison 8% of journeys to work are by rail or Tube and 11% are on foot.

Source: DfT National Travel Survey NTS0409

Family budget

UK households spent an average of £489.00 a week in 2012. This was up from £483.60 a week in 2011.

Transport is the second highest category of household spending after rent, fuel and power for the home, at £64.10 a week. According to the Office for National Statistics, this includes £17.20 on the purchase of vehicles, £36.40 on the operation of personal transport (such as petrol, diesel, repairs and servicing) and £10.50 on transport services (such as rail, Tube and bus fares).

Transport is 13% of the average weekly spend across all households (car owning or not), with vehicle insurance included, it is £74.00 or 15% of the total.

Source: ONS Family Spending

Rural vs urban car travel

87% of rural dwellers (aged 17 or over) are licence holders – compared to 61% for London, and 64% to metropolitan built-up areas.

91% of rural households have at least one car – compared to 55% in London, 67% in other metropolitan areas and the GB average of 75%.

The average rural dweller (all ages, driver or not) does 8,499 miles per year as a car driver or passenger, compared to the GB average of 5,303 miles.

Source: DfT National Travel Survey NTS9901, NTS9902, NTS9904

July 2014

⇨ The above information is reprinted with kind permission from the RAC Foundation. Please visit www.racfoundation.org for further information.

Transport poverty 2014

Poorest households sink deeper into transport poverty.

New figures reveal the least well off families in the UK have slipped further into transport poverty.

Around 800,000 car-owning households spent at least 31% of their disposable incomes on buying and running a vehicle in 2012, the latest year for which official data is available.

In the previous year they spent 27%.

These very poorest families (with the lowest tenth of household incomes in the country) had a maximum weekly expenditure of £167.

Of this £167, £51.40 (31%) went on the purchase and operation of a car.

Of the £51.40:

⇨ £16.40 was spent on petrol and diesel

⇨ £9.50 on insurance

⇨ £6.10 on repairs and servicing

The high proportion of motoring expenditure by those least able to afford it is revealed in data obtained from the Office for National Statistics (ONS) by the RAC Foundation. The previously unpublished numbers were collected as part of the ONS *Living Costs and Foods Survey.*

Professor Stephen Glaister, director of the RAC Foundation, said:

'These figures are definitive. They give the official picture of the financial sacrifices being made by the UK's poorest families to remain mobile.

'Even though there has been some relief at the pumps in recent months and reported falls in insurance prices, it will have done little to ease the burden on those already struggling to make ends meet.

'While record numbers of people now commute by car, including more than half of workers in the most deprived areas of the country, this data shows the cost of transport is a big hurdle to taking up employment.

'For the poorest car owners there is little opportunity to reduce their motoring costs further. They will already be driving as little as they can and will have cut back on things like maintenance. Nor are they likely to be able to afford to swap their car for a newer model with better fuel economy and reliability.

'Before tax we have some of the cheapest petrol and diesel prices in Europe but when you add in fuel duty and VAT the picture changes dramatically.

'The Chancellor rightly points out that he has frozen fuel duty since March 2011 yet almost 60% of the pump price still goes into his pocket.'

To see an interactive chart of how motoring costs have changed over the past decade relative to inflation follow this link:

http://www.racfoundation.org/data/cost-of-motoring-index

The RAC Foundation is a transport policy and research organisation which explores the economic, mobility, safety and environmental issues relating to roads and their users. The Foundation publishes independent and authoritative research with which it promotes informed debate and advocates policy in the interest of the responsible motorist. The Foundation is a registered charity. Number: 1002705.

In December 2013 the Office for National Statistics published the *Living Costs and Food Survey* for 2012. This showed that of average household (car and non-car owning alike) expenditure of £489 per week, transport was the second highest at £64.10 (13%) after housing, fuel and power:

http://www.ons.gov.uk/ons/rel/family-spending/family-spending/2013-edition/index.html

It was upon request that the RAC Foundation obtained from the ONS data relating to car owning households only.

www.racfoundation.org/assets/rac_foundation/content/downloadables/household_expenditure_on_motoring_for_households_owning_a_car_2012.pdf

6 February 2014

⇨ The above information is reprinted with kind permission from the RAC Foundation. Please visit www.racfoundation.org for further information.

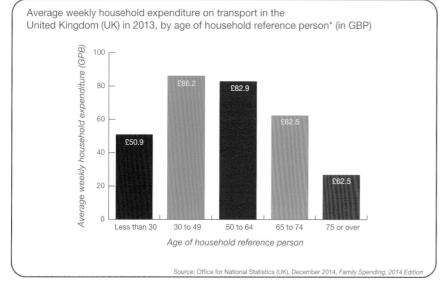

Average weekly household expenditure on transport in the United Kingdom (UK) in 2013, by age of household reference person* (in GBP)

Average weekly household expenditure (GPB)

£50.9 — Less than 30
£86.2 — 30 to 49
£82.9 — 50 to 64
£62.5 — 65 to 74
£62.5 — 75 or over

Age of household reference person

Source: Office for National Statistics (UK), December 2014, *Family Spending, 2014 Edition*

Is your commute to work damaging your health?

According to ONS figures, commuters have higher anxiety levels – and how you travel to work, and for how long, can alter your stress levels.

The ONS survey looked at four factors that define 'personal well-being': life satisfaction, a sense that daily activities are worthwhile, happiness and anxiety, and how these vary based on the length of a person's commute, and the mode by which they travelled.

The figures found that the worst effects of commuting on personal well-being were associated with journey times of between 61 and 90 minutes. The ONS said that 'on average, all four aspects of personal well-being were negatively affected by commutes of this duration when compared to those travelling only 15 minutes or less to work'.

However, when commutes reached three hours or more, the ONS found that the negative aspects began to disappear – and suggested that this could be because people on such long journeys use their time productively.

It might be assumed that people who walk or cycle to work had higher levels of 'personal well-being'. However, the ONS found that the figures varied widely depending on the length of the commute.

Overall, the figures said, people who take a bus or coach to work for more than 30 minutes suffered the most negative effects.

Increased levels of stress have been associated with an increased risk of mortality according to various medical studies, such as this article published in the *British Medical Journal* (http://www.bmj. com/content/345/bmj.e4933).

13 February 2014

⇨ The above information is reprinted with kind permission from Channel 4. Please visit www.channel4.com for further information.

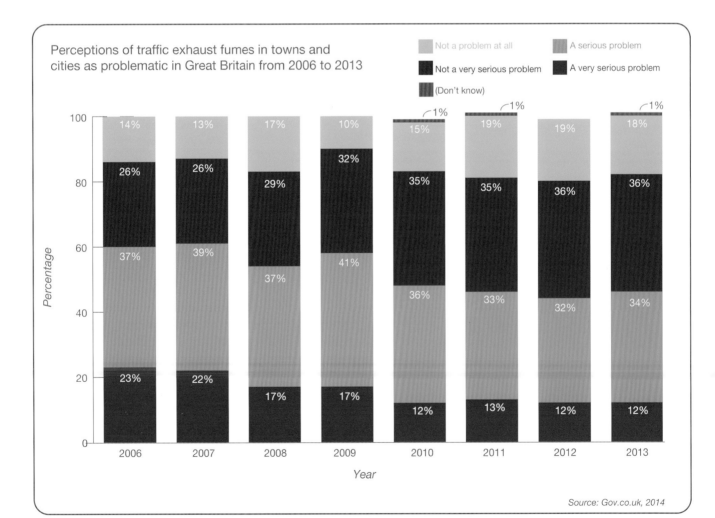

Perceptions of traffic exhaust fumes in towns and cities as problematic in Great Britain from 2006 to 2013

Legend: Not a problem at all | A serious problem | Not a very serious problem | A very serious problem | (Don't know)

Source: Gov.co.uk, 2014

Half of local authorities withdrawing buses after budgets are slashed by 15%

Half of local authorities in England and Wales have cut funding for buses in the current financial year, with over £9 million wiped off support for services.

New research carried out by Campaign for Better Transport shows that since 2010, local authority funding for bus services has been slashed by 15 per cent (£44 million) with more than 2,000 routes being reduced or withdrawn entirely.

Martin Abrams, Public Transport Campaigner, Campaign for Better Transport said:

'Across the country, bus services are being lost at an alarming rate. Year on year cuts to budgets mean entire networks have now disappeared, leaving many communities with little public transport and in some cases none at all. We often hear from people with heart-breaking stories, who have been effectively cut off from society following cuts to their bus service. They are unable to access jobs, shops or public services, and are left in isolation with little contact with the outside world.'

Key findings from the research are:

⇨ Half of English local authorities have reduced funding for bus services in 2014/15. North Yorkshire, Cumbria, Herefordshire, Dorset, Nottinghamshire and Worcestershire are making the deepest cuts

⇨ The overall cut in support for buses in 2014/15 is £9 million. This brings the total reduction since 2010/11 to £44 million – a 15 per cent cut

⇨ Rural areas have been worst hit, seeing average budget reductions of 19 per cent this year

⇨ In 2014/15, nearly 500 bus services were cut, altered or withdrawn, bringing the total to over 2,000 routes since 2010

⇨ 22 Local Authorities have slashed over ten per cent from their bus funding in 2014/15. Seven Local Authorities now don't spend anything on supported bus services

⇨ The overall reduction in Wales in 2014/15 is over £900,000 with 86 bus services having been cut, altered or withdrawn in 2014/15

⇨ A number of authorities are consulting on further major funding reductions in future years. For example, Derbyshire County Council is currently proposing to cut over £2.5 million from its supported bus funding which may include bus routes through the Transport Secretary's constituency.

Martin Abrams said:

'It's very worrying that further steep cuts in budgets are threatened next year and beyond. The Government must wake up to the crisis facing buses and urgently introduce new initiatives which recognise the vital social, economic and environmental role buses play. The challenge for this and future governments is to secure investment in buses and ensure rescue efforts won't be too little too late.'

Campaign for Better Transport is calling on central government to support local buses through the following:

Introduce 'Total Transport' – Total Transport allows existing resources to be allocated and co-ordinated more efficiently resulting in better services for passengers. It works by bringing together the bespoke transport services commissioned by different public bodies – for example inter-hospital link services, social services transport to take older people to day centres, and transport for children with special needs to and between schools. This allows central and local government departments to pool resources and expertise to commission and support transport services including buses. Already popular on the continent, we are calling on the Government to trial Total Transport here.

Fully fund concessionary passes – Nearly 10 million people hold concessionary bus passes, helping to tackle social isolation, encouraging healthy active lives, and contributing to local and national economies. The failure of the Government to fully fund the scheme leaves bus operators at a disadvantage and must be resolved. At the same time it should standardise and enhance concessionary travel schemes for younger people, especially those in education, on apprenticeships or out of work.

Establish a connectivity fund – A connectivity fund should be established to bring together the existing Bus Service Operators' Grant (BSOG) with additional 'top slicing' from 11 other government departments that benefit from functional bus networks such as the Department for Work and Pensions, the Department of Health, Department for Environment Food and Rural Affairs and Department for Education, into a ring-fenced pot for local government to support bus services. The connectivity fund should aim to provide £500 million in bus funding which will pay for itself by reducing the cost of other public services and by supporting economic growth.

12 January 2015

⇨ The above information is reprinted with kind permission from Campaign for Better Transport. Please visit www. bettertransport.org.uk for further information.

Council keeps passengers waiting...
and waiting... for an accessible taxi

Disabled campaigners are calling on a city council to give them a wider choice of public transport, after a five-year delay in deciding whether to license a more accessible type of black cab.

By John Pring

Coventry City Council has been accused of breaching discrimination laws over its long-standing refusal to license larger, more accessible vehicles as taxis.

The council is now one of only five local authorities in England – the others are London, Harlow, Maidstone and Burnley – that are still refusing to license larger vehicles such as the E7, a Peugeot minibus converted to be wheelchair-accessible by Allied Vehicles.

The council claims this is because larger models like the E7 do not have tight-enough turning circles, but critics say the council has delayed making a decision because most of the city's taxis are TX models, manufactured by The London Taxi Company, which is based in Coventry.

A handful of Coventry black cabs are Mercedes-Benz Vito Taxis, which are more spacious than the traditional London cab, but also more expensive and still not as accessible as vehicles like the E7.

Allied Vehicles is now preparing to serve legal papers on the city council over its failure to license the E7, and other vehicles like it.

Allied's legal advisers, Bindmans, believe the council's actions breach its duties under the Equality Act.

Traditional black cabs are not big enough to allow many larger electric wheelchairs to be secured inside the vehicle, with many wheelchair-users forced to travel sideways.

In 2009, a court case established that it was unlawful for a local authority not to take proper account of this safety factor when deciding whether to license larger black cabs, after disabled campaigners took Liverpool City Council to court.

Although there are some accessible private hire minicabs working in Coventry, only licensed black cabs are allowed to use the city's taxi ranks or to be hailed from the side of the road.

Sue Line, acting chair of Coventry Wheelchair User Group, said it was 'very frustrating' that there were still no black cabs that were accessible to disabled people with larger wheelchairs, despite the council spending more than five years considering the proposal.

She said: 'It is up to the licensing authority to make sure that a variety of choice is available.

'I can't understand why they are not licensing other vehicles. They haven't taken on board the variety of wheelchairs that are about.

'The issue is about choice and availability: the ability to hail a cab if you want to.'

Line said she would also like to see a mobile phone application or other source of information so that disabled people had the contact details of private hire and taxi companies in and around the city, and would know which ones were accessible to them.

Last year, consultants produced a report for the council which concluded that the TX taxis prevented larger wheelchairs being secured properly, and that licensing bigger vehicles could improve access for wheelchair-users.

The local authority had been due to discuss the issue last month, but again postponed a decision, and now faces court action.

Simon Guilliatt, market development manager for Allied Vehicles, said: 'If that's what it takes, that's what it takes. We will go to court.'

He added: 'The [taxi-drivers] want to buy [the E7], the wheelchair passengers are happy in them because they have more room and they can travel in the correct manner, but it's just the council not allowing it.'

Cllr Rachel Lancaster, cabinet member for public services, claimed the council had received 'further legal representation which we need to take time to consider'.

She said: 'I know people will be frustrated by the delay but in order to achieve the best outcome for everyone we need to make sure that we have evaluated things fully before a decision is made.'

The council declined to comment further.

13 February 2014

⇨ The above information is reprinted with kind permission from Disability News Service. Please visit www.disabilitynewsservice.com for further information.

© Disability News Service 2015

Boro Taxis firm says disabled passengers will no longer be transported over pricing row

Teesside taxi firm will no longer carry disabled passengers after a row over pricing.

Boro Taxis boss, Mohammed Bashir, said although the decision is 'morally totally wrong', the company can no longer afford to use eight-seater minibuses to pick up a single fare-paying disabled passenger.

Teesside taxi operators were recently told they could lose their licences if they overcharge disabled people after a report found they were often paying double.

He told BBC Tees: 'The simple fact is if you order a car and four people jump in you are charged for a taxi. If you order an eight-seater minibus and eight people jump in you are charged for a minibus.

'If you order a minibus and there's only one person you will still be charged for a minibus because that's what you ordered.

'But because we are charging for a minibus we are breaking the law.'

Middlesbrough Council is investigating the issue.

23 January 2014

⇨ The above information is reprinted with kind permission from the Huffington Post UK. Please visit www.huffingtonpost.co.uk for further information.

Five years on and high-speed rail has 'transformed the economic fortunes of Ashford'

140 mph trains have helped make the international town a Mecca for businesses, residents, retailers and investors.

The UK's only domestic high-speed rail service celebrates its fifth anniversary in December – and for one rapidly expanding Kent town, the 140mph train service 'has transformed its economic fortunes'.

High-speed 1 trains (HS1) slashed journey times from Ashford to the capital by more than half to just 38 minutes when it launched in December 2009.

Five years on and Ashford business leaders say HS1 has given the town a massive competitive edge. 'It has transformed our economic fortunes,' says Cllr Gerry Clarkson, Leader of Ashford Borough Council.

He says the fast train service has attracted businesses and created jobs, improved the quality of life of commuters, drawn more people to live in the Garden of England and has put Ashford in poll position as the place to access London and European markets.

He adds: 'HS1 is the most important economic boost to the South East in years and has strengthened Ashford's reputation as the powerhouse economy of Kent. We have unrivalled road and rail links which, together with highly competitive office and house prices and a dynamic growth agenda, makes the town the smart choice for businesses, investors and residents alike.

'With our connectivity, we have truly now become the only UK international town.'

He said high-speed services have also made a huge difference to Ashford's growing commuter population, 'giving them two hours of their life back every day'.

This popularity is confirmed by operator Southeastern, who say that more than 70% of journeys from Ashford are now made on high-speed trains.

Excellent connectivity is a major reason why Ashford has just been revealed as the best place to do business in Kent, in a poll by inward investment agency Locate in Kent.

The agency's Chief Executive Paul Wookey says: 'Since the introduction of the HS1 services there is no doubt that the perception of Ashford as a business location has improved, as proven in our perception study. It's important that we now capitalise on Ashford's excellent connectivity to London and Europe as the economy continues to improve and levels of inward investment activity increase.'

Expansion of the high-speed service is planned, says Richard Dean, Southeastern's Train

Services Director. 'We will offer a new high-speed "rounder" service from January 2015 that will call at more stations and offer more seats for passengers at key points on our network.

'High-speed has been a really transformational service for rail passengers in East Kent. Its introduction had an impact throughout the region by encouraging more visitors to come to Kent, providing benefits to businesses and by freeing capacity on mainline services as long-distance commuters have moved onto the high-speed trains.

'Capacity is a big issue, and while passengers respond enthusiastically to reduced journey times, which can make a massive difference to their lives, increasing rail capacity also has a big impact on a much greater number of people. Over the next four years we'll be able to expand our high-speed service further, taking it to more stations and opening up journey opportunities for even more passengers,' adds Richard.

Business ranks Ashford as 'the best location in Kent'

According to a recent article in the French newspaper *Le Monde*, a number of French companies have relocated to Ashford in recent years, with all of them citing top class rail links as part of the reason. Electronics after-sales firm SBE, foods supplements specialist Sante Verte, and web TV channel Eclypsia have joined established French employers like perfumes manufacturer Givaudan in making the Kent town their home.

Other big name companies and investors attracted to the town over the past five years include Smith Medical and Verifone (office), Waitrose, John Lewis At Home and Debenhams (retail) and The Document Warehouse (industrial).

Jo James, Chief Executive of the Kent Invicta Chamber of Commerce, says: 'Ashford has always been known for its connectivity and I believe that fast rail services have well and truly put us on the business map.

'We've seen businesses move to Ashford as a result of HS1 and we also know of existing firms who have decided to expand thanks to the introduction of fast trains. I've been contacted by groups involved in the HS2 project keen to know what impact HS1 has had on the economy here and I've told them that it has been an overwhelming success.

'Business needs to be connected and Ashford needs to stay one step ahead of other commercial centres in the UK and Europe if we are to remain successful. Nowhere else in the UK can match our connectivity – we have a network of Eurostar trains to Europe, we are only 38 minutes from central London, 15 minutes from the Channel Tunnel and 25 minutes from Dover Port.'

Jo adds: 'The Government has announced funding for J10a on the M20 and London Ashford Airport has embarked on a multi-million-pound investment as part of their expansion plans at Lydd. The town has had great potential for a long time and, with HS1 in place and a business-friendly local authority driving the growth agenda, we are seeing that potential being delivered.'

According to Tim Allen, a partner at leading development and infrastructure consultancy Peter Brett Associates, Ashford is the only 'mature town' on the high-speed line. Ashford's connectivity makes it the perfect choice, he says, adding that the consultancy made a conscious decision to be situated within walking distance of Ashford International Station.

'Much of our work is client facing and I can receive a call from a client in London in the morning and be with them early afternoon,' says Tim. 'In fact, I often arrive in London more quickly than some of the project partners who are based in the capital.'

More people making Ashford their home

HS1 has also been attracting a steady flow of London property buyers keen to take advantage of Ashford's attractive house prices.

According to Alex Davies, Head of Country Houses at Hobbs Parker estate agents, HS1 is a key factor for property buyers: 'As confidence has come back into the property market in East Kent we are seeing continued interest in HS1 from buyers. The train is a constant in many of our enquiries, especially from people looking to move into the area and with a need or interest in travelling into London regularly,' he says.

'Interestingly, the spectrum of buyers is broader than many predicted when HS1 launched. We are seeing more people who may only need access to London on an irregular basis, from self-employed professionals working mainly from home, to concert musicians, television producers and advertising executives, as well as the newly retired keen to tap into London's culture.

'Along with the traditional commuter, perhaps cashing in a two-bed flat in Islington and needing to get into the City, we are getting increasing numbers of buyers relocating from other, more traditional commuting hotspots, such as Chislehurst, Sevenoaks, parts of Surrey and Essex.'

There is a growing realisation among buyers that by selling a modest home in a traditional commuter belt town and relocating to Ashford they can not only get more property for their money, but also a shorter travel time to work, says Alex.

'There are other incentives too: aside from house price advantages, people are also drawn to our schools, the countryside and good transport links in general, such as the M20 and Eurostar and Le Shuttle services to France,' adds Alex.

'Many of our enquiries are based upon proximity or ease of access to Ashford International, which means certain villages around Ashford are likely to see a degree of price inflation.

'As HS1 opened during the recession, the predicted positive impact on the property market may have been slower than anticipated, but the last couple of years have shown a definite positive effect on both demand and prices in the property market. It may not have been an overnight sensation, but in recent years HS1 has been a significant boost for Ashford and the surrounding area.'

Kevin Hall, Director of estate agents Martin & Co Ashford, agrees HS1 has been a massive draw for property buyers.

'Having a clean, efficient train service that can get into the heart of London in 38 minutes provides a real alternative to people who previously thought they needed to endure stuffy tube journeys from overpriced London properties,' he says.

'We are seeing a broad spectrum of potential buyers from London plus we're being approached by investors who either cannot or do not want to pay London prices. Of course the returns here are much higher and there is less risk given the recent reports of a dangerous property price bubble in London. Buyers are certainly surprised what they can get for their money.

'Londoners and others view Ashford as a good lifestyle choice in addition to the short commute time that HS1 offers. Families are certainly moving to be in a safer environment with better schools. People are also attracted to the possibility of working locally and enjoying a true work-life balance,' adds Kevin.

So has HS1 had a major impact on local house prices?

'Yes and no,' says Kevin. 'Unlike many surrounding towns, Ashford is growing rapidly so ordinarily this would increase supply and have a negative impact on prices. Despite this, demand is still strong so prices are climbing. The overall

effect however is that Ashford remains affordable.'

He also says the current high level of investment and development in the town, backed by the local council's pro-growth policies, is helping to keep demand high.

HS1 has helped transform the lives of many commuters to London, and countless numbers have been drawn to live in Ashford in order to get the most from the fast rail links.

When Lucy Duffy left the capital behind to set up home with her boyfriend in Kent, hassle-free commuting was a big factor in choosing a location. Lucy is Education and Community Project Manager with the London Philharmonic Orchestra, based south of the Thames at Vauxhall. The couple chose a spacious two bedroom flat with a large garden in the town centre, just a ten-minute walk from Ashford International Station.

Lucy, 26, says: 'Property within walking distance of the station is in demand but the rents in Ashford are reasonable and the daily trip to work is so easy. In fact I can usually get to work from Ashford in about the same time as it used to take me travelling between north and south London. And of course the quality of life here in Kent is so much better.'

Tourism and retail boost for Ashford

Quicker train journeys have also helped to attract more tourists to the area, with local hotels reporting more business from the London market. Deirdre Billing, General Manager at Ashford International Hotel, says the reduced journey time has been a key factor for London clients looking for a modern four-star venue without the London price tag.

'Since the launch of the HS1 service, we have seen a massive growth in hotel guests from London and beyond. It has opened up the

---

HS1 fact box

⇨ Southeastern operates 170 high-speed services a day with a half hourly peak time service at Ashford and Faversham. During off-peak periods a service pattern of two trains per hour from Faversham via Gravesend and Ebbsfleet, one from Dover via Ashford and one from Ramsgate via Canterbury West and Ashford applies.

⇨ The trains are Hitachi Class 395 which reach speeds of 140mph

⇨ 8.3% rise in journeys from London (and beyond) into Kent since start of service

⇨ 7.8% increase in journeys from Kent to London (and beyond) since start of service (now at 1.78 million per year)

⇨ 5.6 million journeys into Kent on high-speed since start of service

⇨ On an average weekday 34,000 passengers use high-speed services

⇨ 16% of passengers using high-speed are new to rail

⇨ 93% of high-speed trains reach their destination within five minutes of schedule

⇨ Total journeys (high-speed/mainline) between Ashford and London up by 31%

⇨ More than 70% of journeys from Ashford are now made on high-speed

⇨ Ashford International Station was ranked 134th out of 2,536 in England, Scotland and Wales based on the number of people using it between April 2012 and March 2013 – placing it in the top 6% busiest stations in the UK

Source: Edwards Harvey PR

opportunity to explore Kent, and all the wonderful sights it has to offer,' she says.

McArthurGlen has unveiled plans for the expansion of its Ashford Designer Outlet, which already attracts around three million visitors a year and is located a short walk from Ashford International Station. A planning application is expected to be lodged with Ashford Borough Council soon.

Centre Manager David Maddison says: 'We have seen significant increases in footfall to the centre by people who have travelled by train and consumers who visit us from London are delighted that they can reach us in just 38 minutes. We have big plans for the future of the shopping centre and encouraging people to travel by train plays a large part in our future marketing activity.'

The final word...

Cllr Gerry Clarkson says: 'As we celebrate this landmark anniversary for high-speed rail, we are working hard to build on the success of the service and to ensure that Ashford takes full advantage of all the future opportunities it brings.'

For more information about Ashford visit www.ashfordfor.com

5 November 2014

⇨ The above information is reprinted with kind permission from Ashford Borough Council. Please visit www.ashfordfor. com for further information.

© *Ashford Borough Council 2015*

The case against High Speed 2 (HS2)

Why it's time to think again

High Speed 2 is a flawed government plan to build a new high-speed rail line linking London, the West Midlands, Leeds and Manchester. The total construction cost of the entire project is estimated at £42.6 billion, plus another £8 billion for rolling stock – an unprecedented level of expenditure for a single project ever proposed by a British Government in peacetime. If you agree HS2 is not in the national interest please join us today.

HS2 will be a huge waste of money

The Government's own figures show that returns for Phase 1 (London to West Midlands) have fallen from £2.40 for every £1 of public money spent to £1.40. Comparable figures for the entire network have fallen from £4 to £1.90 for every £1 spent.

But even these figures are suspect – key assumptions on demand, pricing, financing costs and other savings have been manipulated to exaggerate the case for HS2.

Claims that HS2 is needed for capacity don't stack up

The Secretary of State for Transport, the Prime Minister and the vested interests pushing HS2 insist a new line is required to provide additional long-distance rail capacity. They claim that without HS2 our railways will become 'full'.

But the facts are different. The West Coast Main Line is one of our least crowded mainline services and most of its trains have just been lengthened to provide even more seats. Even the most aggressive forecasts for future demand can be met by improving existing lines and worst of all, HS2 does little to address the real problem of overcrowding on commuter lines in London, Birmingham, Leeds, Manchester and Glasgow.

HS2 will be an environmental catastrophe

HS2 will have a devastating impact on wildlife and some of our most precious landscapes and ecosystems. Over 130 protected wildlife sites are impacted by Phase One alone.

The new line would also increase carbon emissions – with official figures showing few passengers transferring from road (8%) or air (3%) to rail, and instead many new journeys being created.

HS2 creates few jobs and is London-centric

Creating jobs is crucial to the British economy and its recovery – but HS2 is not the answer. Official figures confirm the project will create few jobs and those which are created will overwhelmingly be based in London.

The benefits for London are likely to be magnified given the route choice of HS2, which will not permit journeys between our great northern cities. HS2 will not be an option for direct travel between Liverpool, Leeds, Manchester and Newcastle, but will instead encourage trips to London.

The scheme's backers claim HS2 is a 'done deal' – but this is far from correct. A broad coalition of economic, environmental and other groups, plus thousands of people who have come together as registered supporters of HS2AA, are fighting to make the case against HS2. To join us, sign up here: http://www.hs2actionalliance.org/sign-up/.

⇨ The above information is reprinted with kind permission from HS2 Action Alliance. Please visit www.hs2actionalliance.org for further information.

© *HS2 Action Alliance 2015*

Global status report on road safety 2013

Executive summary from the World Health Organization report.

Road traffic injuries are the eighth leading cause of death globally, and the leading cause of death for young people aged 15–29 (1, 2). More than a million people die each year on the world's roads, and the cost of dealing with the consequences of these road traffic crashes runs to billions of dollars (3). Current trends suggest that by 2030 road traffic deaths will become the fifth leading cause of death unless urgent action is taken (2).

Strategies exist that are proven to reduce road traffic injuries and a number of countries have successfully used these strategies to reduce their road traffic deaths. In 2004, the World Health Organization (WHO) and the World Bank launched the *World report on road traffic injury prevention* (4). The World report provides extensive information on leading risk factors for road traffic injuries and evidence on effective interventions, and makes recommendations to countries on how to improve national road safety. Progress in implementing the recommendations of the *World report* was first reported in the *Global status report on road safety: time for action* (2009) (5).

In 2010 the United Nations General Assembly unanimously adopted a resolution calling for a Decade of Action for Road Safety 2011–2020, and for further *Global status* reports on road safety to monitor the impact of the Decade at national and global levels. This report builds on the 2009 report, and provides additional data in a number of important areas. It serves as the baseline for monitoring the Decade.

The report shows that there has been no overall reduction in the number of people killed on the world's roads: about 1.24 million deaths occur annually. However, this plateau should be considered in the context of a corresponding 15% global increase in the number of registered vehicles, suggesting

that interventions to improve global road safety have mitigated the expected rise in the number of deaths. 88 countries – in which almost 1.6 billion people live – reduced the number of deaths on their roads between 2007 and 2010, showing that improvements are possible, and that many more lives will be saved if countries take further action. However, of concern is that 87 countries saw increases in the numbers of road traffic deaths over the same period. The report also shows that the highest road traffic fatality rates are in middle-income countries, particularly the African Region. More than three-quarters of all road traffic deaths are among young males. The report notes the need for standardised data collection on fatalities and the need for improvement in the quality of road safety data on road traffic deaths, non-fatal injuries and disability. It also stresses the importance of good postcrash care, both in terms of providing quick access for road traffic victims to health care, and in ensuring the quality of trained hospital trauma

care staff in mitigating the negative outcomes associated with road traffic crashes.

The first *Global status report on road safety* highlighted the lack of comprehensive legislation on key risk factors (speed, drink–driving, motorcycle helmets, seat-belts and child restraints) for road traffic injuries (5). Between 2008 and 2011, 35 countries, representing almost 10% of the world's population, passed laws to address one or more of these five key risk factors. The action taken by these countries to implement new laws indicates that – with country commitment – progress is possible. However, there has been no increase in the number of countries with adequate legislation on all five key risk factors – the 28 countries (representing 7% of the world's population) with comprehensive laws remain unchanged from the last evaluation in 2009. The report also highlights that enforcement of these laws, which is critical to their success, is inadequate.

The report serves as a strong warning to governments to address

the needs of non-motorised road users. 27 per cent of all road traffic deaths occur among pedestrians and cyclists. In low- and middle-income countries, this figure is closer to a third of all road deaths, but in some countries is more than 75%. As the world continues to motorise, walking and cycling need to be made safe and promoted as healthy and less expensive mobility options. However, only 68 countries have national or subnational policies to promote walking and cycling, and just 79 countries have policies that protect pedestrians and cyclists by separating them from motorised and high-speed traffic. Although governments increasingly recognise the need to promote alternative forms of mobility, more emphasis needs to be given to making these modes of transport safe. Addressing the safety of pedestrians, cyclists and motorcyclists is critical to successfully reducing the total number of global road traffic deaths.

The report further highlights the important role that road infrastructure can play in reducing injuries among all road users, including pedestrians, cyclists and motorcyclists. It recommends that governments implement regular road safety audits to assess safety levels of both existing and new road infrastructure projects. The report also outlines progress that has been made to implement minimum vehicle safety standards, and encourages governments to work with vehicle manufacturers to ensure that ever-larger proportions of their fleets meet these standards.

Real progress has been made towards improving road safety and saving lives, but what this report shows is that faster and more concerted action is needed to prevent many more lives being needlessly lost on the world's roads. Therefore the report makes the following recommendations:

⇨ Governments urgently need to pass comprehensive legislation that meets best practice on all key risk factors to address this preventable cause of death, injury and disability.

⇨ Governments should invest sufficient financial and human resources in the enforcement of these laws, as an essential component for their success. Raising public awareness can be an important strategy in increasing understanding of and support for such legislative and enforcement measures.

⇨ Concerted effort is needed to make road infrastructure safer for pedestrians and cyclists. The needs of these road users must be taken into consideration earlier, when road safety policy, transport planning and land use decisions are made. In particular, governments need to consider how non-motorized forms of transport can be integrated into more sustainable and safer transport systems.

References

1. Murray CJL et al. Global and regional mortality from 235 causes of death for 20 age groups in 1990 and 2010: a systematic analysis for the Global Burden of Disease Study 2010. *Lancet*, 2012, 380:2095–2128.

2. Global burden of disease, 2008. Geneva, World Health Organization, 2011(http://www.who.int/healthinfo/global_burden_disease/ estimates_regional/en/index.html, accessed 22 February 2013).

3. Jacobs G, Aeron-Thomas A, Astrop A. Estimating global road fatalities. Crowthorne, Transport Research Laboratory, 2000 (TRL Report 445).

4. Peden M et al., eds. World report on road traffic injury prevention. Geneva, World Health Organization, 2004 (www.who.int/violence_injury_prevention/publications/road_traffic/world_report/en/index.html, accessed 22 February 2013).

5. Global Plan for the Decade of Action for Road Safety, 2011–2020. Geneva, World Health Organization, 2011 (www.who.int/roadsafety/decade_of_action/plan/plan_english.pdf, accessed 24 January 2013).

2013

⇨ The above information is reprinted with kind permission from the World Health Organization. Please visit www.who.int for further information.

Public Health professionals call for 20mph limits

Public Health leaders are increasingly identifying wide-area 20mph limits as key for liveability and health equality. Speed reduction tackles risk, inactivity, obesity, isolation and is child, disability, elderly and dementia friendly.

The Royal College of Paediatrics and Child Health & National Children's Bureau advocate Total 20 in built up areas.[1] Their *Why Children Die* research, led by Dr Ingrid Wolfe found around 2,000 additional children per year – five a day – die in the UK compared to Sweden. Over three quarters of injury deaths in 10–18-year-olds are due to traffic incidents. Reducing the national speed limit in built up areas to 20mph is a key recommendation for child protection to cut the source of daily road risk. More than 80% of child road casualties occur on 30mph limited streets.

As well as these direct safety gains, 20mph limits promote health and well-being in many other ways:

⇨ By encouraging a shift to walking, which reduces obesity and heart disease

⇨ Lower emissions promote healthier lungs

⇨ Increased mobility for children and the disabled, elderly or dementia sufferers delivers gains in health and self-esteem

⇨ Better inclusion and access to society for non-car owners and greater equality for the poor

⇨ Up to 50% reduction in noise from road traffic

⇨ Less congestion from 'school run' and other trips as people choose to move from car-based journey to more active ones by walking and cycling

⇨ Increased social cohesion and less loneliness as people talk to each other far more on less traffic dominated streets.

Birmingham's Director of Public Health Dr Adrian Phillips said: 'We talk a lot about obesity and the need for people to be more physically active but we have to take action to make that easier. It's vital that people feel safe on the roads. Creating safer, more attractive walking and cycling routes through reducing the speed limit to 20mph will significantly increase numbers of walkers and cyclists and contribute towards a mode shift away from cars to active travel. Removing barriers to walking and cycling will reduce health inequalities and provide a foundation for the citywide promotion of active travel through smarter choices initiatives.[2]'

20mph limits is the top evidenced based policy to raise regular exercise levels according to a Public Health England and LGA report. In *Obesity and the environment: increasing physical activity and active travel*,[3] Dr Nick Cavill and Professor Harry Rutter recommend 20mph as the best way to improve exercise by raising walking and cycling levels.

Professor Danny Dorling, from Oxford University is author of a 20mph chapter in the British Academy's health inequality collection.[4] He said: 'I was asked to provide the evidence base for a single workable policy to reduce inequalities in public health. Reducing car speeds does this in a way that is far more directly obvious than any other single health policy. The effects range from reduction in casualties, right through to the

encouragement of more healthy walking and cycling when people are less afraid of fast cars in their neighbourhoods. The cost is minimal and the benefits are enormous.'

All *Take Action on Active Travel*[5] report partners including the Association of Directors of Public Health, Faculty of Public Health and UK Public Health Association want 10% of transport budgets allocated to active travel and 20mph speed limits in towns and villages. 'Make 20mph or lower speed limits the norm for residential streets and those used by shoppers, tourists and others, close to schools or public buildings, or important for walking and cycling or children's play. In urban areas only the busiest strategic traffic routes should now qualify for higher speed limits.'

And in Liverpool City Council, Manchester City Council, Calderdale Council and Lancashire Council the community benefits are seen as so important that Public Health teams have supported implementations of wide-area 20mph limits with direct funding. Healthy roads have slower speeds. Write to your Local Health Cabinet Councillor and Public Health lead today to work towards 20mph with transport colleagues.

May 2014

⇨ The above information is reprinted with kind permission from 20's Plenty for Us. Please visit www.20splentyforus.org.uk for further information.

© 20's Plenty for Us 2015

1   http://www.rcpch.ac.uk/system/files/protected/page/WhyChildrenDieFINAL.pdf 1 May 2014

2   http://birminghamnewsroom.com/2014/04/health-boss-welcomes-20mph-limit/ 30 April 2014

3   PHE https://www.gov.uk/government/publications/obesity-and-the-environment-briefing-increasing-physical-activity-and-active-travel Nov 2013

4   http://www.britac.ac.uk/policy/Health_Inequalities.cfm "If you could do one thing.." guide for Local Authorities 16 Jan 2014

5   http://www.fph.org.uk/uploads/Take_action_on_active_travel.pdf Sustrans 2008

UK Conservatives defend right to break speed limit

On 2 September 2014, Conservative MEPs put their foot down on EU attempts to fit cars and vans with hi-tech devices to stop them breaking the speed limit following UK press reports that they were in the pipeline.

The European Commission said there were no concrete plans, however, insisting that the results of a stakeholder consultation into the issue had not yet been finalised.

Intelligent Speed Adaptation works using satellites, which communicate limits to cars automatically, or using cameras to read road signs, to automatically adjust the speed of the vehicle.

'Under the proposals new cars would be fitted with cameras that could read road speed limit signs and automatically apply the brakes when this is exceeded,' reads a report in the *Sunday Telegraph* from 1 September.

The *Mail on Sunday* said that UK transport minister Patrick McLoughlin had instructed his officials to block the move because they 'violated motorists'' freedom.

Big brother behind the wheel

'Even Big Brother didn't try remote control of people's cars. I don't know whether this is an imminent threat or a gleam in some Commission official's eyes, but if or when it appears before the Transport Committee I can assure you Conservatives will be down on it like a ton of bricks,' said Conservative transport spokesperson Jacqueline Foster, MEP for the UK's North-West.

'It is also an insult to personal freedom to say that bureaucrats in Brussels are effectively going to have their foot on your brake pedal.

Britain has the best road safety record in Europe and we won't have it compromised by nonsense like this,' Foster concluded.

A spokeswoman for the European Commission said that the reports 'may be referring to the stakeholders' consultation held in the framework of the study on speed limiters'.

Such automatic speed limiters are currently fitted to heavy goods vehicles and buses. The consultation will assess the effectiveness of the limits and consider extending the devices to cars and vans.

'There is no legislative proposal in preparation concerning Intelligent Speed Adaptation. This will have to wait until the study results are available, which will be some time before the end of the year,' said the Commission spokesperson.

Positions:

A spokesman for the UK Automobile Association said that a recent poll by the group showed 43% in favour of mandatory automated speed limiters but 49% against.

'We noticed that there are some downsides; it tends to encourage speeding on roads which are not covered by ISA and can lead to reduced attention, not found in a voluntary system,' the AA spokesman said.

⇨ The above information is reprinted with kind permission from EurActiv.com. Please visit www.euractiv.com for further information.

Air travel is safe and getting safer – whatever else you might have read

An article from The Conversation.

By Simon Bennett

THE CONVERSATION

If you've been following the news it might seem like there's been a lot of air crashes recently. It might seem that flying has become a risky business.

In a society with a free press and a great number of publications, the likelihood that bad things will happen can be overstated to the point where the public begins to think and act irrationally. Nick Pidgeon, Roger Kasperson and Paul Slovic describe this phenomenon in their 2003 book, *The Social Amplification of Risk*, where individuals, social groups or institutions such as the press act as 'amplification stations', heightening or dampening certain aspects of the message leading to different interpretations.

For example, the disappearance of Malaysia Airlines flight MH370, the shooting down of Malaysia Airlines flight MH17, the loss of Air Algérie flight AH5017 and most recently Air Asia flight QZ8501: the hyperbolic reporting surrounding these events can induce feelings of dread. *In extremis*, a routine activity such as hopping on a plane can become stigmatised to the point where the facts and figures surrounding its relative safety are misinterpreted or ignored.

As another example, in the energy sector far more workers are killed mining coal than are killed operating nuclear power plants. Yet because of the association of civilian nuclear power with nuclear weapons, and because of the stigmatisation of nuclear power generation from the 1960s onwards – amplified by accidents such as Three Mile Island, Chernobyl and Fukushima and environmentalists' media-savvy campaigns – many believe the opposite to be true.

In the same way that a handful of nuclear accidents had an outsize influence on the perception of nuclear energy's safety, so the loss of flights MH370, MH17, AH5017 and QZ8501 have influenced how safe people perceive commercial aviation to be.

The numbers don't lie

This has led to, and is fuelled by, headlines such as 'After MH17 And Two Other Plane Crashes, Is It Still Safe To Fly?' and many others in a similar vein. Aviation journalist David Learmount observed: 'The 2014 Malaysian disasters... have twisted perceptions of airline safety.' The subsequent loss of AirAsia flight QZ8501 in the last days of December will only have heightened those concerns.

However, despite these high-profile disasters and the media coverage around them, last year was one of the industry's safest. According to Flightglobal's report, last year's global fatal accident rate of one per 2.38 million flights makes 2014 the safest year ever, following one accident per 1.91 million flights in 2013, one per 2.37 million in 2012, one per 1.4 million in 2011 and one per 1.26 million in 2010.

According to the Aviation Safety Network, of aircraft carrying more than 14 passengers and excluding sabotage, hijacking and military accidents, in 2014 there were 20 crashes accounting for 692 fatalities – one of the lowest accident rates on record, even if the number of casualties is up on recent years, the highest since 2010.

So why do we think the opposite? Roughly one-third of passengers are what the industry calls 'nervous flyers', who tend to assume the worst. The academics suggest that individuals either dampen or amplify risk signals. Some find the thought of not being in control unnerving, others are content to trust the unknown strangers – pilots, controllers, dispatchers, loaders, fuellers, engineers, regulators – who make it possible. Trust issues induce negativity. The tone of post-disaster newspaper headlines, especially those in many tabloids, border on alarmist. Such hyperbole is also capable of influencing some people.

It's true that flying is not without risk: flying several hundred people tens of thousands of feet above the ground at close to the speed of sound in an environment subject to turbulence and low temperatures (-55°C) in a pressurised aluminium tube packed with fuel and potential ignition sources simply cannot be without risk. Fortunately, thanks to the superhuman efforts of those working at the daily grind of commercial aviation, flying is remarkably safe.

Following the 11 September attacks in 2001, many Americans stopped flying. This switch to *terra firma* produced a spike in transport-related deaths. Why? Because flying is safer than almost every other mode of transportation. Had the defectors stuck with aviation there would have been fewer deaths. Ironic. By far and away the most risky form of transport is by motorcycle, which is more than 3,000 times more deadly than flying. Travelling in a car or truck is about 100 times more dangerous, while taking the train is twice as deadly as flying.

Clearly, failing to perceive where the real risk lies, or misconceiving risk where there is none, can have deadly consequences. It is not flying that kills, but fear of flying.

15 January 2015

⇨ The above information is reprinted with kind permission from The Conversation. Please visit www.theconversation.com for further information.

Europe's cycling economy has created 650,000 jobs

Cycling industry employs more people than mining and quarrying with potential for a million jobs by 2020, says new study.

Europe's cycling industry now employs more people than mining and quarrying and almost twice as many as the steel industry, according to the first comprehensive study of the jobs created by the sector.

Some 655,000 people work in the cycling economy – which includes bicycle production, tourism, retail, infrastructure and services – compared to 615,000 people in mining and quarrying, and just 350,000 workers directly employed in the steel sector.

If cycling's 3% share of journeys across Europe were doubled, the numbers employed could grow to over one million by 2020, says the *Jobs and job creation in the European cycling sector* study which will be published next month.

Kevin Mayne, the development director at the European Cyclists' Federation (ECF) which commissioned the paper, said that it had a very simple message for governments and local authorities: 'You know that investing in cycling is justified from your transport, climate change and health budgets. Now we can show clearly that every cycle lane you build and every new cyclist you create is contributing to job growth. Investing in cycling provides a better economic return than almost any other transport option. This should be your first choice every time.'

'This report is another example of the way that a transformation to a green, low-carbon economy can create jobs with the appropriate investment,' Julian Scola, a spokesman for the European Trade Union Confederation told *The Guardian*. 'There needs to be investment in various kinds of transport infrastructure, including cycling.'

The study, which *The Guardian* has seen, finds that cycling has a higher employment intensity than any other transport sub-sector.

Growth in the cycling economy should thus have a higher job creation potential than in the automotive industry for example, which employs three times less people per million euros of turnover.

Surprisingly, the lion's share of jobs in the new free-wheeling economy are in bicycle tourism – including accommodation and restaurants – which employs 524,000 people, compared to 80,000 in retail, the next highest sub-sector.

New innovations such as e-bikes, as well as road safety campaigns, and infrastructure projects could boost the cycling economy further according to the ECF, which wants 10% of Europe's transport budget to be set aside for cycling.

In general, cycling jobs are more geographically stable than other sectors, and offer a more inclusive and easily accessible labour market for low-skilled workers, says the new report, which was produced by the Transport and Mobility Leuven research institute.

The study also signals some unexpected knock-on benefits that bikes can have for local businesses. Cycling 'contributes probably more to the local economy than the use of other transport modes', because 'cyclists go more to local shops, restaurants, cafes than users of other transport modes', the paper says.

12 November 2014

⇨ The above information is reprinted with kind permission from *The Guardian*. Please visit www.theguardian.com for further information.

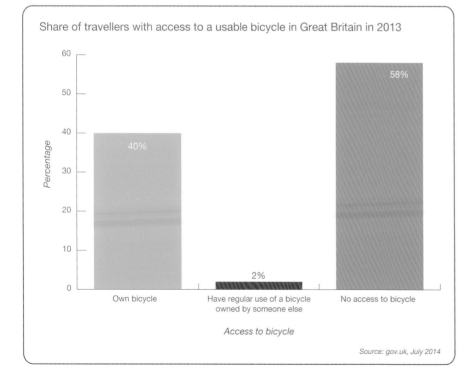

Share of travellers with access to a usable bicycle in Great Britain in 2013

- Own bicycle: 40%
- Have regular use of a bicycle owned by someone else: 2%
- No access to bicycle: 58%

Access to bicycle

Source: gov.uk, July 2014

High-quality traffic-free routes encourage more walking and cycling

The provision of new, high-quality, traffic-free cycling and walking routes in local communities has encouraged more people to get about by foot and by bike, according to a new study published today in the American Journal of Public Health.

Two years after new routes were developed by charity Sustrans with local authority partners, people living nearby increased their total levels of physical activity, compared to those living further away.

People living 1km (0.6 miles) from the new routes had increased their time spent walking and cycling by an average of 45 minutes per week more than those living 4km (2.5 miles) away.

This could make a substantial contribution to helping people achieve the two-and-a-half hours of physical activity per week recommended by health experts.

Independent research led by the MRC Epidemiology Unit at the University of Cambridge, on behalf of the iConnect consortium, surveyed adults living in three communities before and after they benefited from a national initiative led by the sustainable transport charity Sustrans, and funded by the Big Lottery Fund, to build or improve walking and cycling routes at 84 towns, cities and villages around the UK.

Crucially, there was no evidence that the gains in walking and cycling were offset by reductions in other forms of physical activity. This suggests that the new routes have encouraged local people to become more active overall. The benefits were equally spread between men and women and between adults of different ages and social groups. However, people without access to a car were more likely to increase their activity levels than those who had a car.

Dr Anna Goodman, lecturer at the London School of Hygiene and Tropical Medicine and lead author of the paper, said: 'These findings

support the case for changing the environment to promote physical activity by making walking and cycling safer, more convenient and more attractive. The fact that we showed an increase in overall levels of physical activity is very important, and shows that interventions of this sort can play a part in wider public health efforts to prevent diabetes, heart disease and other chronic conditions.'

Dr David Ogilvie of the MRC Epidemiology Unit at the University of Cambridge, who led the study, added: 'Although it may seem intuitive that improving facilities for walking and cycling will help make the population more active, this has rarely been tested in practice, and most of the existing studies have been done in other parts of the world. This is one of the first studies to show that changing the environment to support walking and cycling in the UK can have measurable benefits for public health. It is also notable that we did not see a significant effect on activity until two-year follow-up. It can take time for the benefits of this sort of investment to be fully realised.'

Malcolm Shepherd, Chief Executive of charity Sustrans who implemented the three projects with support from the Big Lottery Fund, said: 'It's clear that when good quality infrastructure exists people use it. Our experience from co-ordinating the National Cycle Network, which saw an amazing three quarters of a billion (748 million) journeys in 2013, 7% more than the year before, has shown us this over and over again.

'With a physical inactivity crisis and traffic jams clogging our towns and cities the case has never been stronger for governments to guarantee dedicated funding for

quality walking and cycling routes for everyone.'

Peter Ainsworth, Chair of the Big Lottery Fund added: 'In 2007, Sustrans' Connect2 project won the public TV vote to bring £50 million from the Big Lottery Fund to communities across the UK to create networks for everyday journeys for people travelling by foot or bike. The study released today showcases brilliantly the long-lasting benefits that this transformational funding is achieving in creating greener, healthier, fitter and safer communities.'

The three communities studied were in Cardiff, where the centrepiece of the project was a new traffic-free bridge across Cardiff Bay; Kenilworth in Warwickshire, where a new traffic-free bridge was built across a busy trunk road to link the town to a rural greenway; and Southampton, where a new boardwalk was built along the shore of the tidal River Itchen. All of these new crossings then linked into extensive networks of routes.

17 July 2014

⇨ The above information is reprinted with kind permission from Sustrans. Please visit www.sustrans.org.uk for further information.

Walking, cycling and public transport beat the car for well-being

Walking or cycling to work is better for people's mental health than driving to work, according to new research by health economists at the University of East Anglia and the Centre for Diet and Activity Research (CEDAR).

The research reveals that people who stopped driving and started walking or cycling to work benefited from improved well-being. In particular, active commuters felt better able to concentrate and were less under strain than if they travelled by car.

These benefits come on top of the physical health benefits of walking and cycling that are already widely documented.

Experts also found that travelling on public transport is better for people's psychological well-being than driving.

Lead researcher Adam Martin, from UEA's Norwich Medical School, said: 'One surprising finding was that commuters reported feeling better when travelling by public transport, compared to driving. You might think that things like disruption to services or crowds of commuters might have been a cause of considerable stress. But as buses or trains also give people time to relax, read, socialise, and there is usually an associated walk to the bus stop or railway station, it appears to cheer people up.'

The research team studied 18 years of data on almost 18,000 18–65-year-old commuters in Britain. The data allowed them to look at multiple aspects of psychological health including feelings of worthlessness, unhappiness, sleepless nights, and being unable to face problems. The researchers also accounted for numerous factors known to affect well-being, including income, having children, moving house or job, and relationship changes.

The study also shows commute time to be important.

Adam Martin said: 'Our study shows that the longer people spend commuting in cars, the worse their psychological well-being. And correspondingly, people feel better when they have a longer walk to work.'

Data from the 2011 Census (England and Wales) shows that 67.1 per cent of commuters use cars or vans as their usual main commute mode compared to 17.8 per cent who use public transport, 10.9 per cent who walk and just 3.1 per cent who cycle.

'This research shows that if new projects such as the £5.7 million "Push the Pedalways" programme of cycling improvements in Norwich, or public transport schemes such as the busway in Cambridge, were to encourage commuters to walk or cycle more regularly, then there could be noticeable mental health benefits.'

The new report contradicts a UK Office of National Statistics study *Commuting and Personal Well-being, 2014*, published in February, which found people who walked to work had lower life satisfaction than those who drove to work, while many cyclists were less happy and more anxious than other commuters. Crucially, this new research looks at commuters who had changed travel mode from one year to the next, rather than comparing commuters who were using different travel modes at a single point in time.

The research was carried out by the Health Economics Group at UEA's Norwich Medical School and the Centre for Health Economics at the University of York. It was funded by CEDAR, a multi-disciplinary collaboration between UEA, the University of Cambridge and MRC Units in Cambridge.

15 September 2014

⇨ The above information is reprinted with kind permission from the Centre for Diet and Activity Research (CEDAR). Please visit www.cedar.org.uk for further information.

Lack of dedicated routes leaves pedestrians at risk from cyclists

An article from The Conversation.

By Akshat Rathi

THE CONVERSATION

Governments around the world are pushing to get their citizens to cycle more. Without necessary infrastructure, however, that is not good news for pedestrians or cyclists.

While on an evening stroll, no one likes a bike whizzing past on the same footpath. Many pedestrians worry about getting injured by cycles more than by cars, and their perception of risk in this case is not much off the mark. Data reveals that in the UK cyclists are nearly as likely to cause a serious injury to a pedestrian as motorists are.

The absolute number of people hurt by cyclists is quite small, but so is the corresponding distance travelled by cyclists. Thus the relative risk from cyclists and motorists is comparable.

According to British government data, between 2003 and 2012, cyclists killed 23 pedestrians and injured 585, whereas motorists killed 4,894 and injured 45,496. But in 2012, motorists cover as much as 50 times the distance in urban areas as cyclists do. Using corresponding casualties data, the relative risk from motorists to pedestrians is five times as much as that from cyclists if the injury leads to death, but the risk of seriously injuring a pedestrian is about the same.

The data is comparable to that acquired from Transport for London (TfL), the city's authority for all matters vehicular, through a freedom of information request by the National Cycling Charity. The request was to find out how much cyclists hurt pedestrians on footways only. (In legalese footway is one that runs alongside a carriageway, whereas a footpath is located away from it.)

In the period from 1998 to 2007, cyclists killed none and caused some injury to 98 pedestrians on footways in London. For motorists, the corresponding numbers were 54 and 4,460. If the distance travelled by motorists is assumed to be about 50 times that of cyclists, like the 2012 national average, the relative risk of causing some injury to pedestrians is nearly the same from cyclists as it is from motorists.

However, John Parkin, Professor of Transport Engineering at the University of West England, said, 'Provisions for cyclists are so appalling that it is not surprising some find it easier and safer on the footway. If cyclists need to go on pedestrian routes, then the Government needs to provide better infrastructure.'

According to Parkin, the last decade has seen improvement in cycling infrastructure, at least in cities like London, but much remains to be done.

One solution being backed by Network Rail, operator of most British rail infrastructure, and TfL is the development of SkyCycle – a 220km car-free route installed above London's suburban rail network. But, as Steven Fleming and Angelina Russo write on The Conversation, many cyclists are not too impressed by this initiative. For the price tag of £220 million, many argue there are cheaper ways to improve matters.

Compared to the rest of Europe, the UK has among the smallest proportion of people using cycles as their main means of transport. Only about two in 100 Britons fall into that category, which is marginally better than Bulgaria, Malta and Cyprus.

Politicians want to change that. An all-party inquiry is considering how best to get Britons cycling. Hopefully they will heed the advice of not just cyclists but also pedestrians.

23 January 2014

⇨ The above information is reprinted with kind permission from The Conversation. Please visit www.theconversation.com for further information.

Study shows where on the planet new roads should and should not go

Researchers have created a 'large-scale zoning plan' that aims to limit the environmental costs of road expansion while maximizing its benefits for human development.

More than 25 million kilometres of new roads will be built worldwide by 2050. Many of these roads will slice into Earth's last wildernesses, where they bring an influx of destructive loggers, hunters and illegal miners.

Now, an ambitious study has created a 'global roadmap' for prioritising road building across the planet, to try to balance the competing demands of development and environmental protection.

The map has two components: an 'environmental-values' layer that estimates that natural importance of ecosystems and a 'road-benefits' layer that estimates the potential for increased agriculture production via new or improved roads.

The authors of the new study, recently published in the journal *Nature*, write that by combining these layers they have identified areas where new roads have most potential benefit, areas where road building should be avoided, and conflict areas 'where potential costs and benefits are both sizable'.

'It's challenging but we think we've identified where in the world new roads would be most environmentally damaging,' said co-author Professor Andrew Balmford from the University of Cambridge's Department of Zoology.

'For particular regions the approach can be improved by adding detailed local information but we think our overall framework is a powerful one.'

'Roads often open a Pandora's Box of environmental problems,' said Professor William Laurance of James Cook University in Australia, the study's lead author. 'But we also need roads for our societies and economies, so the challenge is to decide where to put new roads – and where to avoid them.'

Professors Laurance and Balmford worked with colleagues from Harvard, Cambridge, Melbourne, Minnesota and other universities for nearly two years to map out the world's most important ecosystems and biodiversity.

After mapping out the priority areas for conservation, the team then tried to decide where roads would have the greatest benefits for humanity.

In general, areas that would benefit most from new roads are those that have largely converted to agriculture but are currently relatively low-yielding but not too distant from urban markets. All continents have regions that fit this bill – including parts of central Eurasia, Central America and Mexico, and the Atlantic region of South America.

'We focused on agriculture because global food demand is expected to double by mid-century, and new or improved roads are vital for farmers,' said Dr Gopalasamy Reuben Clements from James Cook. 'With better roads, farmers can buy fertilisers to raise their yields and get their crops to markets with far less cost and waste.'

'The good news is that there are still expanses of the world where agriculture can be greatly improved without large environmental costs,' said Dr Nathan Mueller of Harvard University, USA.

Areas with carbon-rich ecosystems with key wilderness habitats, such as tropical forests, were identified as those where new roads would cause the most environmental damage with the least human benefit, particularly areas where few roads currently exist.

'Our study also shows that in large parts of the world, such as the Amazon, Southeast Asia, and Madagascar, the environmental costs of road expansion are massive,' said Christine O'Connell from the University of Minnesota, USA.

The authors emphasise that there will be serious conflicts in the coming decades.

'We're facing a lot of tough decisions,' said Irene Burgues Arrea of the Conservation Strategy Fund in Costa Rica. 'For instance, there are huge conflict areas in sub-Saharan Africa, because it has vital wildlife habitats but a very rapidly growing human population that will need more food and more roads.'

The study's authors say that this new global road-mapping scheme can be used as a working model that can be adapted to for specific areas. They say that proactive and strategic planning to reduce environmental damage should be central to any discussion about road expansion.

'We hope our scheme will be adopted by governments and international funding agencies, to help balance development and nature conservation,' said Professor Laurance.

'So much road expansion today is unplanned or chaotic, and we badly need a more proactive approach. It's vital because we're facing the most explosive era of road expansion in human history,' he said.

Given that the total length of new roads anticipated by mid-century would encircle the Earth more than 600 times, the authors point out that there is 'little time to lose'.

28 August 2014

⇨ The above information is reprinted with kind permission from the University of Cambridge. Please visit www.cam.ac.uk for further information.

Labour's drive towards diesel cars causing 'massive public health problem', admits Shadow Environment Minister

Fuel linked to higher levels of air pollution deaths, say experts.

By Jonathan Owen and Jamie Merrill

The drive by the previous Labour government to encourage millions of Britons to opt for diesel cars in a bid to save the planet was 'wrong' and a 'massive problem for public health' Barry Gardiner, Shadow Environment Minister, has admitted.

Ten million Britons drive diesel cars, in a trend which was encouraged by tax breaks given by Gordon Brown when he was Chancellor of the Exchequer.

Last year more than half of all new cars sold were diesel. But while they may have lower CO_2 emissions than their petrol counterparts, diesel cars emit a higher amount of deadly pollutants – including nitrogen dioxide and sooty particulate matter – which have contributed to dangerous levels of air pollution resulting in the deaths of 29,000 people a year.

Compared to petrol cars, diesels produce 22 times the amount of particulate matter – a cause of cancer linked with the premature deaths of thousands of Britons each year. And they emit up to four times more nitrogen oxides – including nitrogen dioxide, which damages lungs and blood vessels and can cause heart disease, stroke and diabetes.

Barry Gardiner MP, Shadow Minister for the Environment, said: 'Hands up, can I say there's absolutely no question that the decision we took was the wrong decision, but, and it is a big but, at that time we didn't have the evidence that subsequently we did have and we had cleaner diesel engines, which we thought meant that any potential problem was a lower grade problem than the problem we were trying to solve of CO_2.'

Speaking in a *Dispatches* documentary being broadcast on Channel 4 tomorrow evening, he claims the drive for diesel was the 'right move away from those vehicles who were pushing out CO_2 emissions'. But Mr Gardiner admits: 'Certainly the impact of that decision has been a massive problem for public health in this country.'

He adds: 'The real tragedy is after we set up the committee on the medical effects of air pollution and it reported back in 2010 we've had five years that this government has done nothing about it.'

But government ministers were warned of the risks more than 20 years ago, according to Professor Roy Harrison, professor of environmental health at the University of Birmingham: 'I chaired an advisory committee in 1993 who was advising government on urban air quality issues and we recognised that there might be future problems associated with the increasing uptake of diesel passenger cars.'

And air quality is so poor that it is stunting the lungs of young children in parts of London, according to preliminary findings from research by experts at Queen Mary University Hospital and Kings College, London. Professor Chris Griffiths, QMUL, said: 'When we look at the lung development of children who have been exposed to the highest levels of pollution compared with the lowest levels of pollution they are developing smaller stunted lungs, and that's a big concern.'

The documentary also reveals how car drivers are exposed to higher levels of diesel pollutants than cyclists and pedestrians.

Professor Frank Kelly, Chair of the Committee for the Medical Effects of Air Pollution, says: 'When people are in cars if they've got windows closed and the air conditioning on, they probably think that they are actually immune from the emissions from the vehicles in front of them and in reality that's not the case because the gases penetrate so easily that they will get into the cabin of the vehicle and depending on the ventilation of that cabin they may actually build up to much higher concentrations.'

And Alan Andrews, lawyer, ClientEarth, said: 'I think people have been conned to some extent. People still think diesel is the green fuel and buying a diesel car they are doing the right thing by the planet. The truth is diesel is a very heavily polluting fuel: certainly from a public health point of view we can't have dirty diesels in our towns and cities.'

Legal limits of nitrogen dioxide were exceeded in 40 of Britain's 43 urban zones, according to the latest government report on air quality.

In London, local councils are already pushing back against diesel engines, with plans in Islington and Hackney for a surcharge on parking permits for diesel vehicles.

Islington Council has been using its emission-based parking system to encourage a shift to diesel cars since 2007, but now diesel car owners will have to pay an extra £96 a year.

Elsewhere in the capital, diesel drivers in Camden and Kensington and Chelsea already pay up to £18 extra a year for older diesel vehicles. The Mayor, Boris Johnson, also plans to raise the congestion charge for diesel cars by £10.

The British car industry has reacted with dismay to the 'blanket' clampdown on diesel by local councils. One source close to Ford, which recently opened a new £190 million diesel engine plant at Dagenham, said the firm and wider industry viewed it as the start of a 'demonisation of diesel'.

Mike Hawes, the chief executive of the Society of Motor Manufacturers and Traders (SMMT), said: 'Blanket polices which fail to distinguish between modern clean [diesel] vehicles and decades-old technologies are not the solution.' He added: 'The decision to impose new financial penalties on diesel owners who bought their cars in good faith is unreasonable and demonstrates a concerning lack of understanding about the huge technological advances that are already making diesel vehicles cleaner.'

But Alan Andrews, ClientEarth, told *The Independent on Sunday*: 'Legal limits for air pollution are being broken by huge margins in towns and cities up and down the country and that's largely down to diesel.'

In a statement, a government spokesperson said: 'This government has invested heavily in measures to help tackle the issue of air quality, committing £2 billion since 2010 to increase ultra-low emission vehicles, sustainable travel and green transport schemes, as well as promoting walking and cycling. We are working with businesses and the public health sector to promote understanding and encourage action to further reduce exposure.'

25 January 2015

⇨ The above information is reprinted with kind permission from *The Independent*. Please visit www.independent.co.uk for further information.

How car sharing is encouraging green habits beyond taking cars off the road

By Romy Rawlings

Gone are the days when an automobile was the ultimate desirable luxury. The concept of proud sole ownership is being eroded by the concept of car sharing and the mobility experience has been opened up through joint-use, which allows consumers to share certain items instead of owning them. Car ownership, and its inherent responsibilities, has been replaced by the idea of eco-mobility, smarter choices and the possibility of renting cars whenever we want, for as long as we like. Sharable transportation is not just a smart way of dealing with our real-time demands, it's also a valid solution to the problem of congested and polluted streets.

In an attempt to spur innovation and transform existing public transport, cities around the world are introducing car-share programmes, aiming to reduce the need to own a car. As we continue to explore trends behind shared space and schemes like bike-sharing, we move on to investigate the benefits of car share. In this article we look at how 'mobility on demand' is becoming a cost-competitive solution.

What is car sharing?

The principle behind sharing a car is to persuade the public to replace their own cars with easy and cheap mobility options that could be viewed as attractive travel resources. These schemes aim to open up possibilities to those who are interested in reducing carbon emissions and want to help combat climate change. For a younger generation, who are less interested in owning their own personal transport, car sharing is a way of keeping the car at bay and discouraging its unnecessary use. For those in rural areas, car clubs are an extension of the transport network, allowing access to relatively nearby locations that are often just out of reach for public transport.

But car sharing is more than just a trend that combats the oil and energy crisis. It's a continuation of a collaborative consumption shift which is taking over the world. Sharing allows us to rediscover values that our society seems sometimes to have forgotten: trust, and the borrowing and lending of goods.

The uncomplicated 'Book, Unlock, Drive and Pay' service reflects the trends and flexibility of today's lifestyle, and the shifting character of our careers. The new world of digital technology is enriching our choices through websites, smartphones and mobile apps which, in just a few clicks, make it possible to book car-sharing services, unlock and drive away with the use of a smart card. Car sharing makes journeys around cities an easy experience, where modern travellers can hire a car whenever they want and for as long as they need to. The car is easily accessed within walking distance of a transport interchange and, after use, it can be parked and paid for based on the calculated time usage. No insurance, tax, maintenance costs, or parking fees are involved in this new mode of mobility.

In 2010 a new approach to car sharing was introduced: peer-to-peer car sharing. This is a form of person-to-person car lending where an existing car owner makes their vehicle available for others to rent for a short period of time. This form of car sharing was pioneered in the US by ZipCar, and was quickly adapted by peer-to-peer car clubs all over the world. The system doesn't only have potential for city-dwellers either: the easyCar Club in Linlithgow, Scotland, provides car owners with the opportunity to make extra money from something they already own, and are paying for. This creative distribution of goods is another sign of our willingness to push forward the idea of a shared economy.

Another form of car sharing is carpooling, also known as lift-sharing, which encourages sharing journeys together with more than two people. This form of joint-use concept originates from the US and was initially established as a rationing tactic during World War II. Nowadays, services like BlaBlaCar, Carbon Heroes, GoCarShare and Liftshare, are making travelling with strangers along the same route a much cheaper and more environmentally friendly experience.

Car sharing is a step closer to a sustainable transport vision

The first pay-as-you-go car-sharing programme was introduced in Switzerland and Germany and in the UK, car-sharing programmes – commonly known as car clubs – have been gradually gaining recognition since 1999. Subsequently, many successful car club schemes – City Car Club, Streetcar, Connect by Hertz, ZipCar, Co-wheels and others – have been established, and even supported by government funding. The Department for Transport (DfT) has funded 48 car clubs and car-sharing schemes through the Government's Local Sustainable Transport Fund.

Carplus, a national transport charity which promotes car clubs across the UK, plays a leading role in promoting low-carbon alternatives to traditional car use. The organisation has been awarded £500,000 by the DfT to help expand and develop successful car club schemes across the country.

This more affordable and sustainable form of transport is

also available to the less able. BCC (Bristol Car Club) offers wheelchair accessible car hire which is adapted to carry wheelchair users and up to four other passengers. Their minibus hire system is accessible on hourly, daily or weekly hire to charities and social enterprises in and around Bristol, making commuting and social access a more readily available solution.

A wave of new car sharing is storming Germany, the home of the automobile, where the first car was invented. Affordable short-term rental has suddenly overtaken the idea of ownership, changing the stakes for Germany's 'favourite child'. Suddenly car-sharing has become so popular that almost half of 8.5 million one-way car shared trips booked around the world last year happened in Germany.

The German automobile industry is not falling behind this trend, instead it is offering alternative systems and a chance to rent a car which some would never be able to afford. Big manufacturers like Mercedes, Daimler and BMW have joined this transition by supplying and fulfilling Germany's collaborative needs with various car-sharing programmes such as Car2Go, DriveNow and Quicar. Even Germany's railway company Deutsche Bahn supports the joint-use concept, with various car rental models as a way of closing the gap that is often the last mile of citizens' journeys.

In France, car ownership is also undergoing a transition in attitude. As a solution to crowded streets and lack of parking spaces, France has launched the world's most sophisticated car-sharing networks. The car-sharing companies offer convenient, yet much cheaper, solutions to owning a car which are perfectly in line with the vibrant French web-sharing economy. It's also worth noting that Paris has the world's largest electric car share programme – 'Autolib' – which was launched in 2011.

Car-sharing has even emerged in China as part of a sustainable strategy aimed to reduce high levels of air pollution and traffic congestion. China, home to 1.351 billion people, has, over the past two decades, developed an unhealthy love affair with the automobile, which escalated due to the growing demand for personal mobility and an increase in overall wealth. As a drastic solution to these problems, Chinese cities introduced car-sharing schemes to instigate a shift away from this car-centric culture and foster better awareness of the role of urban transport.

Car sharing has many benefits:

⇨ 'Around 30% of Scottish car club members decreased their annual mileage by an average of 3,546 miles, while 22% increased it by on average of just 1,051 miles' (Research by Carplus)

⇨ According to GOV.UK there is evidence which suggests that pay-as-you-go car use encourages people to walk and cycle more often and make more frequent use of public transport.

⇨ 'In London each car club car displaces between six and 17 private vehicles, with car sharers reporting driving fewer miles using more efficient vehicles, saving more than 2,260 tonnes of carbon each year.' (Research by Carplus)

⇨ According to GOV.UK, car clubs can help save irregular drivers money – potentially around £3,500 a year.

How car sharing is becoming ever more popular

As a political and environmental battle continues to shift people away from using cars towards alternative modes of transport, car-sharing schemes seem to have a major impact on people's automobile use. In many cities around the world, where an average vehicle is only used for around 45 minutes a day, a car rental membership could open the doors to more conscious and efficient car use.

As traffic congestion in cities across the UK worsens every year (according to research by TomTom), so improving and expanding public transport will be essential. The rapid demand to make our cities greener and healthier is raising the profile of collaborative consumption which comes with another benefit: it saves money too.

9 September 2014

⇨ The above information is reprinted with kind permission from Marshalls. Please visit www.marshalls.com for further information.

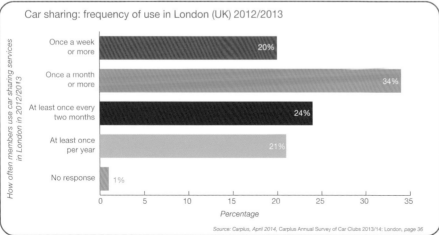

Car sharing: frequency of use in London (UK) 2012/2013

How often members use car sharing services in London in 2012/2013

- Once a week or more: 20%
- Once a month or more: 34%
- At least once every two months: 24%
- At least once per year: 21%
- No response: 1%

Percentage

Source: Carplus, April 2014, Carplus Annual Survey of Car Clubs 2013/14: London, page 36

Electric vehicle FAQs

The thought of driving an electric vehicle may throw up a few questions: 'How do I charge it?', 'Where do I charge it?' and 'How long will it take to charge?'.

By Vicki Mitchem

The good news is that changing your fuelling habits is an easy (and convenient) adjustment to make, thanks to the rapidly expanding charging network. With over 7,000 electric charging points across the UK in October 2014, and nearly 300 added in the last 30 days, electric vehicle infrastructure in the UK is growing at quite a pace. It's a remarkable rate of growth, which looks set to rise. What's more, given the impressive range of many electric vehicles, such as the BMW i3 Range Extender that's capable of covering up to 180 miles, you could find that you're taking less time out of your week to refuel.

Types of charge points

There are broadly three different rates of charging. Standard charging that takes up to eight hours, Fast charging that can fully charge an i3 in less than three hours, 0–80%, and Rapid charging that provides 80% charge in just 30 minutes. The optional DC Rapid charge function is the perfect solution for the BMW i3, allowing you to charge and go at compatible DC Rapid charging stations.

The ChargeNow network

BMW i, which includes the award-winning BMW i3 and the progressive BMW i8 sports plug-in hybrid, operates ChargeNow, the UK's largest network of charging stations, allowing BMW customers access to flexible and time-saving charging points in public locations such as car parks and city centres. ChargeNow combines charging stations from various charge point operators into one expansive network, allowing you to charge your car at any of the partner charging stations and receive just one monthly bill.

BMW i drivers can find their nearest ChargeNow charging stations in their car, or online, both of which are automatically updated with live availability.

For an annual fee of £20 and pay-as-you-go billing, payment is simple and cashless via the ChargeNow card. You register a card with us and the costs are billed on a monthly basis.

Charging at home

As many privately owned vehicles are parked at home overnight, it's only natural that this is the time most electric vehicles are charged, ensuring they are ready for use the next day. Charging at night utilises electricity supplies when they are least in demand and cost less, and it's also convenient, ensuring you don't have to take time out to stop and recharge. Many owners of electric vehicles opt to have a charge point installed at home, ideally where the vehicle is parked off-street, such as a driveway, garage or car port. At present an OLEV Government subsidy is available that covers up to 75% of the purchase and installation costs for Electric Vehicle owners. Suppliers of home charging equipment will be able to provide you with more detailed information on this.

Every BMW i vehicle comes with a cable that allows you to charge the high-voltage battery from a conventional socket, but for regular Fast charging the BMW i Wallbox Pure is recommended as a convenient home solution. This AC Fast charging system can take less than three hours to charge from 0 to 80%, and thanks to funding costs just £360*.

* Subject to subsidy approval (available throughout all the UK, including Northern Ireland), and includes telephone survey, standard 32A installation and three-year warranty.

Source: BMW

10 October 2014

⇨ The above information is reprinted with kind permission from *Securing the Future*. Please visit www.securingthefuture.co.uk for further information.

Towards an all-electric future?

We take a look at some exciting developments in electric vehicles, and whether they can really offer a sustainable long-term alternative to the petrol/diesel ones.

Following the recent World Car-Free Day, when people are traditionally asked to leave their cars at home, Climate & Us takes this opportunity to talk to Martin Elliott, EDF Energy's man with an electric van, about a different kind of car.

You've been working on electric vehicles (EVs) for a few years now. How do progress and innovation compare to the expectations you had when you started?

When I joined the team about three years ago, despite being a keen car enthusiast, I didn't know much about electric vehicles. The thing that struck me straight away was how good they are to drive. They use regenerative braking, which harnesses energy that would otherwise be lost and uses it to increase the range of the car. It is really impressive, and together with the instant power from the electric motor, it adds to the pleasurable and relaxed driving feel.

From driving early prototype vehicles such as the MINI E back in 2012, I have seen how rapidly the technology has progressed since then. The latest production vehicles are refined, practical and desirable. Advances in battery technology and the use of heating and cooling systems on the cars has increased the efficiency of the vehicles and extended the driving range. You can also now charge them quicker and connect remotely through smart technology to switch the charging on or off and pre heat or cool the car before you even go out to the vehicle.

What have been the main triggers for progress in that area?

As more manufacturers begin to look at electric technology it increases the number of people working in this field. This increases the knowledge and skills base and also brings down the costs associated with their development and production as the products become more mass market rather than low volume niches.

Investment funding from the Government in schemes relating to low carbon vehicle technology, vehicle purchase subsidies and charging infrastructure grants have all helped play a part.

Carbon emission reduction from transport is a key topic on the agenda around the world and more time and money is being spent on it. We are seeing multinational collaboration into research and development to share the knowledge and spread the cost.

Sales of electric cars are booming – registrations have more than doubled in the first half of 2014. Could you talk us through the different types of car available?

It is really encouraging to see the figures about booming sales, and even more encouraging to actually see the vehicles on the road. Driving home yesterday I saw four on my journey from Brighton to London, and that's not including the one I was driving!

I purchased a Nissan Leaf earlier this year as my own personal car. The Leaf is a full battery EV which means that there is no petrol/diesel engine on board, and it can only be fuelled with electricity.

For those people that may need to go a little further from time to time, a range-extender may be more suitable. This type of vehicle has a petrol or diesel powered generator on board that produces more electricity to propel the vehicle until such time that it can be plugged in again.

A third type of electric vehicle is a plug-in hybrid. This type can be powered by electricity obtained by plugging into the mains, or powered by a petrol/diesel engine when the electricity has run out. They typically have a lower 'electric only' range than the range-extender, and the other main difference is that the petrol/diesel engine propels the vehicle

IT TOOK AGES TO GET USED TO THE QUIETNESS AND THE CLEAN AIR!

THE SKY... IT'S SO BLUE!

when running, whereas the range-extender is always propelled by the electric motor.

Can you see electric cars ever becoming mainstream? Or do you think the future lies with other fuels?

I believe that the future of transport will be a mixture of technologies. This will certainly include electric power but it won't be the sole fuel, and I see things such as hydrogen also playing a part.

Electric cars are at a stage now when they are starting to become more mainstream. They are now being put together with petrol and diesel vehicles in showrooms and motor show stands, rather than being singled out as something different.

Public recognition and acceptance is also growing and I think over the next couple of years people will start to give serious consideration to them when making a new vehicle purchase decision.

What do you think will be the single most important thing needed for that to happen?

The single most important thing that I believe will increase EV sales is purchase price reduction. At the moment they are more expensive than an equivalent petrol/diesel and this really puts a lot of people off. Over the whole life of a vehicle an EV can be a lot cheaper than running a combustion engine (cheaper to fuel, no road tax, no congestion charge, lower maintenance, less BIK tax for company car drivers) but people don't realise that and only see the higher purchase price.

However, things are starting to change on that front and a really significant milestone has been achieved recently by Mitsubishi. They have priced their new Outlander plug-in hybrid at the same price as the diesel equivalent. As a result they are seeing record sales and hopefully this could be the catalyst for other manufacturers to follow suit.

How much pressure would a wholesale adoption of electric vehicles (and the building of the necessary charging network) put on the UK electricity grid? And how much carbon savings would it actually deliver?

The ideal scenario for owning a plug-in vehicle is being able to charge it at home (for the public) or at a work location (for businesses). This way the recharging can be done overnight when there is spare capacity on the grid and generally cheaper tariff prices for using it.

Public charging such as on streets and in car parks is a good tool to give reassurance to people that they could top up while out if needed. However, research figures show that by far the majority of charging is done at home and work.

Overall carbon savings and ability to provide energy rely on a low carbon grid mix and it's vital that the energy supplies around the world are decarbonised as much as possible to realise the benefits of electric vehicles.

You've been working with manufacturers, and organising quite a few test drives around EDF Energy's offices, giving employees the opportunity to try the cars for themselves. What's the reaction like on the whole?

Reaction to these events has been fantastic. The test drive slots were all snapped up within 24 hours of being announced and interest on the day at the sites has been great. We've seen crowds of people looking at the cars, asking questions, sitting in them and taking photographs. It's been really nice for me to introduce electric vehicles to a new audience and to talk directly with people to dispel any misconceptions they may have. I have also had a couple of people say to me that they would now seriously consider an EV when buying a new car, whereas before the event they wouldn't have.

And finally, what do you think is the most exciting electric vehicle right now?

There are two cars that I see as exciting developments and possible game changers in the EV market. Firstly is the BMW i8 sports car which has just been launched. This is one of the best looking cars around and coupled with the incredible driving performance, is providing an inspirational halo car for plug-ins.

Secondly is the Tesla Model 3 which is currently still in development. With this car Tesla are aiming to bring performance and prestige at a lower price. The product pricing is being targeted at the executive car sector of the market and could lead to rapid growth of electric vehicles amongst this high volume sales area.

25 September 2014

⇨ The above information is reprinted with kind permission from Climate&Us. Please visit www.climateandus.com for further information.

© EDF ENERGY 2015

People-oriented cities: smarter driving, smarter cities

The 'People-oriented Cities' series – exclusive to TheCityFix and Insights – explores how cities can become more sustainable and liveable through transit-oriented development (TOD). The nine-part series addresses different urban design techniques and trends that reorient cities around people rather than cars.

By Claudio Sarmiento and Marco Priego

The more cars on the road, the more challenges a city faces. Developing countries like Mexico have experienced increased car ownership in recent years, as much as 23 per cent annually since 1995. As these car-owners take more trips, there are more road fatalities, traffic congestion, longer commuting times, and air pollution. Despite these risks, most cities are decidedly car-centric and rely on private vehicles for almost all urban trips, whether or not a car is the most efficient or convenient option.

Creating safer, more sustainable cities means designing them to move people, not cars. One way to achieve this goal is transport demand management.

What is transport demand management?

Transport demand management refers to a set of strategies that maximise urban mobility by limiting the unnecessary use of private cars. These strategies recognise that cars will always play a role in the make-up of a city, and work to manage car use by promoting more sustainable and integrated transport options. Furthermore, they make streets safer for all commuters – drivers, cyclists and pedestrians.

To get anywhere in a city, travellers decide what mode of transport to

use, which route to take, and which is the most convenient way to go. Transport demand management focuses on each of these links within a city's transport system, cutting car-dependence and making sustainable transport more attractive.

Build up sustainable mobility options

Car-oriented cities are sprawling and dispersed, leaving a disproportionate amount of space for cars at the expense of other modes of transport. Even with carpool lanes and car-sharing schemes, which use road space more efficiently, private cars still gridlock city streets. For example, it takes up to 50 times more road space for cars to carry the same number of people as the average public transport vehicle in Mexico City, based on the city's average occupancy of 1.21 passengers per car.

But without viable alternatives, commuters are left with few options beyond the car. The availability of public transport that connects people's homes to schools or employment centres can make for a better, shorter commute and reduce traffic congestion, as everyday commutes make up nearly 30% of total vehicle traffic in North American cities.

Integrate car travel with other forms of transport

Cars can be an efficient piece of urban transportation systems, but only if integrated with more sustainable modes like bus rapid transit (BRT), metro, and active transport. Commuters can easily drive to a designated car park and take public transport or walk to their destinations. These park-and-ride or park-and-walk programmes have proven to be successful before sporting events such as the 2011 Pan-American Olympics in Guadalajara, where only ten per cent of attendees parked outside the main stadium.

Design safer streets

Street design is also a key factor. Car-oriented cities are designed to move vehicles at high speeds. While this makes motorised mobility convenient, it also increases the risk of traffic crashes, inhibits access to other means of transport, and endangers pedestrians and cyclists.

Better street design can minimize road safety risks and slow cars down without hindering their flow. City speed limits work: New York City's inner-city speed limit of 25mph (40km/h) is more fuel-efficient and prevents 80 per cent of collisions from being fatal. Traffic calming measures also help create safer streets by reducing speeds:

⇨ Narrowing vehicular lanes, covering surfaces with rough paving, and adding speed bumps

⇨ Prioritising pedestrian crossings by extending pavements or raising roadway surfaces at junctions

⇨ Providing clear traffic signals for all road users.

Regulate parking

Making parking inexpensive and easy spurs the demand for cars. Free parking subsidises driving and encourages car-centric development, fuelling urban traffic congestion and road safety risks. Cities can reduce car dependence by:

⇨ Controlling the supply of parking spaces based on land use and available transport alternatives instead of projected increases in parking demand

⇨ Charging for parking for more efficient use of space

⇨ Prioritising space for sustainable transport alternatives such as car-share stations, bicycle parking and bus stops.

People-oriented cities recognise the car as part of a larger sustainable mobility strategy, and must therefore provide solutions to adequately manage car use. Transport demand management can improve city-dwellers' quality of life, but only if local governments, urban planners, and other stakeholders apply these strategies in conjunction with complementary urban mobility strategies. In the end, the smartest city is not the one that eliminates cars, but the one that can integrate them into a sustainable network of urban mobility options.

13 August 2014

⇨ The above information is reprinted with kind permission from Responding to Climate Change (RTCC). Please visit www.rtcc.org for further information.

Driverless car concept gains traction with young people

Four in ten under-40s would be interested in having a driverless car, though British people tend to think they won't catch on.

By Will Dahlgreen

When Google first experimented with driverless cars, they added sensors and a computer to a Toyota Prius and allowed humans to override it if they wanted to. Afterwards, however, they said they 'saw stuff that made us a little nervous'. Now, they say completely driverless cars – with no steering wheel or pedals – will be much safer. As one commentator put it: 'Humans might be the one problem Google can't solve.'

A new YouGov survey finds a mixed public reception for driverless cars.

Overall, 60% say they would not buy a driverless car, even if money were no object. Though a significant minority (30%) say they would, and the figure is much higher among 18–39-year-olds (39%) than over-40s (26%).

Future tech

Previously, YouGov found that 60% also said they would not buy a smartwatch if money were no object, a project Google are also now thought to be working on.

But while people did tend to think smartwatches would catch on, by 46–34%, they are not fully convinced driverless cars will do the same. 51% predict they will not become popular, while 37% say they will. However, younger adults once again provide more reason for optimism about the future of the technology. Those between the ages of 25 and 39 tend to believe driverless cars will catch on by 48–42%.

Google plans to build a fleet of 200 experimental electronic driverless cars. The two-seat vehicle will, to begin with, be limited to 25mph, and will come with plug-in controls that the company hope to remove when confidence grows. They claim the cars could revolutionise transport, by making roads safer, eliminating crashes, and decreasing congestion and pollution.

30 May 2014

⇨ The above information is reprinted with kind permission from YouGov. Please visit www.yougov.co.uk for further information.

From locating potholes to monitoring air quality, new technologies could revolutionise the UK's transport system and reduce local authority costs

A new guide launched on 6 October 2014 by the Institution of Engineering and Technology (IET) and Intelligent Transport Systems (ITS) will help local authorities make use of new technologies, such as big data analytics and cloud computing, to revolutionise their local transport systems while also reducing costs.

In the current political and financial environment, where local authorities are increasingly strapped for cash, the guide illustrates how some local authorities have used technology to improve their transport systems while managing, and in some cases reducing, costs.

The guide sets out some of the advantages new technologies can bring in solving existing and future transport problems. Examples range from smartphone apps to determine road and cycle path conditions, to Bluetooth systems that allow transport operators and planners to analyse journeys across multiple transport modes

in near real-time. It also discusses some of the important issues when implementing these new solutions, including open standards, security and privacy issues.

Potentially dramatic changes in procurement as travel and transport systems become increasingly based around Internet technologies are also outlined. Traditional methods of ownership and operation can be replaced by buying systems as services, relying on cheap communications media such as remote hosting or 'cloud' solutions.

Also highlighted in the guide are some local authorities who are already embracing new technologies. These include:

⇨ Dublin City Council, using smartphones and tablets to better manage traffic technology

⇨ Sunderland City Council, working with the Met Office, to run a transport and weather information pilot to improve traffic and travel throughout the region

⇨ Hampshire County Council, introducing a smarter street lighting system for over 100,000 lights and signs, which has reduced Hampshire's CO_2 emissions by 4,000 tonnes – the equivalent to the CO_2 emitted from 1,600 cars per year

⇨ Milton Keynes City Council, from December 2014, replacing its existing diesel buses with a new fleet of electric buses that will run seven days a week

Miles Elsden, Acting Chief Scientist, Department for Transport, says: 'Given today's challenging financial environment, local authorities are finding it increasingly difficult to deliver the transport systems that people need. This new guide gives a comprehensive overview of the potentially cost-saving new technologies available for local transport, which will hopefully encourage more local authorities to take a fresh approach to the way to plan and procure for transport in the future.'

Alison Carr, Director of Governance and Policy at the Institution of Engineering and Technology explains: 'Recent advances in transport technologies offer excellent opportunities for local authorities to deliver transport services more effectively and efficiently – but there are a number of barriers to overcome, from lack of awareness of what is possible to the need for new, more flexible procurement.

'This guide aims to open local authorities' eyes to the new world of possibilities out there when it comes to developing their transport systems – and to the opportunities new technologies present to reduce costs.'

6 October 2014

Driverless cars could change lives for disabled people, if we let them

An article from The Conversation.

By Catherine Easton and Heather Bradshaw

THE CONVERSATION

With testing already happening in the US and trials given the green light in the UK, the autonomous car seems like more of a possibility than ever. Aside from the early adopters who want to be part of the newest technology trend, the autonomous car has enormous potential to help those who, for whatever reason, can't drive themselves.

We've seen over the past few decades that technology can have a transformative effect on the lives of disabled people. But these benefits can only be realised if the technology itself is designed and regulated with the needs of all users in mind.

The Internet, for example, makes new ways of communicating possible, but it needs to be designed in an accessible manner. All kinds of new technologies have sprung up, such as screen readers that transcribe audio content so that websites can be used by disabled people.

And it's not just disabled people who stand to benefit. With an ageing population across the Western world, the potential for new technology to enhance the lives of those whose capabilities may differ from an accepted norm needs to be embraced at an early stage.

Effective transport can be crucial to achieving a full life. Research indicates that disabled people can often feel isolated through lack of access to effective transport services. Targeted schemes and policies can help but they don't provide the same level of independence as when someone is able to choose exactly where they go.

This is exactly where autonomous cars can make a difference. But whether people who can't drive will start using them is linked to the attitude of society as a whole towards the new technology. Only once they are accepted as safe will they become a viable option for the elderly and disabled people.

This, in turn, is connected to the nature of the technology and how certain concepts are defined. The most important will be our definition of the word 'driver' – even if we mean to get rid of them entirely – and whether we decide that an autonomous car needs to have at least one human driver on board in case something goes wrong.

International law describes a driver as 'any person' who should 'at all times' be 'able to control' the vehicle. If a disabled person were, today, to travel in a fully autonomous system, there would still be a need for an additional passenger 'able to control' the vehicle, even if his or her presence were entirely passive.

Potential solutions to this include assigning a level of 'personhood' to the systems controlling the car and thereby fulfilling the legal requirement for a 'driver' to be a 'person'.

While this solves one problem, it raises ethical and legal questions about who is actually responsible for the car. There are potential implications for the people who actually develop the systems in the first place, for example.

Another solution might be to develop systems akin to air traffic control. Cars could be monitored from a central location and could be over-ridden if the need arose. This would solve all kinds of problems but would be difficult to achieve in terms of infrastructure and might pose some extra dilemmas about privacy.

A third solution would be to push for an amendment to international legal framework governing road use in order to redefine the concept of 'driver' to include inanimate systems. Amending the provisions of the relevant conventions is not unprecedented and could stand as an important move towards updating the law in light of technological change.

The prospect of autonomous cars is exciting for everyone, but for some, it could be life changing. There are all kinds of questions we need to answer before we see these machines on our roads but in answering them, we should consider how to legislate to make this an opportunity for everyone. We need to think through all the potential scenarios so we can produce a robust, future-proof, ethical legal environment that works for a range of people – be they drivers or passengers.

These are not just fun gadgets, they could bring a whole new way of getting around to people who are at the moment excluded to varying degrees. Let's make sure they aren't forgotten on the road to automation.

(Heather Bradshaw also contributed to this article, based on her research in the field of autonomous car ethics.)

13 August 2014

⇨ The above information is reprinted with kind permission from The Conversation. Please visit www.theconversation.com for further information.

Driving into the future (with the brakes on)

Vehicles will continue to become more connected and more automated, and we will increasingly manage our journeys through our smartphones, says Kevin McCullagh.

By Kevin McCullagh, Founder of Plan

The future of transport looks bright following two recent announcements. First, Mayor Boris Johnson unveiled a sleek new design for London Underground trains, which will be faster, cooler, driverless and Wi-Fi-enabled... in 2025. Meanwhile, in California, Elon Musk – inheritor of Steve Jobs' mantle as hero of Silicon Valley – yanked back a satin sheet to reveal three new Tesla models of electric car; one does 0–60 in 3.2 seconds, as well as driving itself into the garage and automating much of motorway driving.

The milestones of mobility history are marked by the coverage of greater distances in faster, cheaper, safer and more convenient ways. Mass car ownership, cheap flights and high-speed trains have broadened our minds and life experience more than any previous generation. So what are the prospects for transport over the next 20 years? Will innovation continue to drive us into a zippier future? I believe it will, but with a major caveat: even as exciting innovations spark progress, there is a widening gap between mass aspirations for more speed and comfort, and the agenda of transport planners who are steering with their foot on the brakes.

This is particularly the case with urban transport. Some planning projects are truly ambitious, such as Crossrail, which will whisk Londoners from Heathrow to Canary Wharf in 40 minutes by 2018. But the future also holds plenty of attempts to constrain speed and convenience, nudging us into bike sharing or shoving us into congestion charging, pedestrianisation and rationed parking. (Hamburg, for example, plans to banish cars from 40 per cent of its centre by 2032.)

What these plans don't take into account is the aspirational desire for fast, cheap, convenient transport. It's often said Generation Y has fallen out of love with car ownership – a perception that has pleased the planners and worried car companies. But while the recession and student debt may have delayed young peoples' car-buying plans, all of our research confirms that the young still aspire to their own wheels – and the freedom and individuality a car still represents.

When the Estonian capital of Tallinn recently became the largest city to give its residents free access to public transport, this European centre for nightlife – with a huge young population – saw only a one per cent rise in usage, mostly from walkers, not drivers, making the switch. Drivers are attached to the comfort and convenience of their transport, a fact planners often dismiss.

Innovation will happen more at individual level – vehicles and smartphones – rather than much more costly large-scale civic planning and infrastructure.

What won't happen

Two darlings of the urban visionaries are car sharing and electric vehicles (EVs). While both will find their niches, neither will mainstream as the planners hope. Car clubs like ZipCar promise car access over the hassle of ownership and have been promoted by many city authorities. However, the Mercedes-backed Car2Go recently withdrew from a pilot in the UK in the face of public disinterest – many

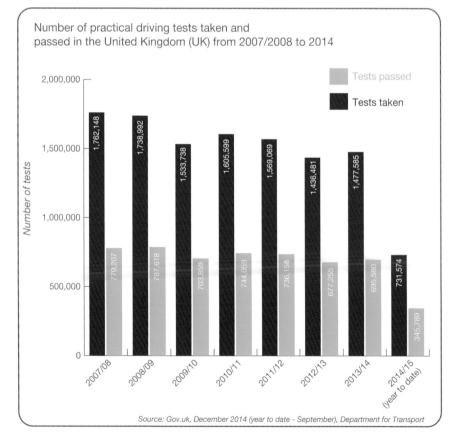

Number of practical driving tests taken and passed in the United Kingdom (UK) from 2007/2008 to 2014

Tests passed
Tests taken

Number of tests

2,000,000

1,500,000

1,000,000

500,000

0

2007/08: 1,762,148 / 779,207
2008/09: 1,738,992 / 787,618
2009/10: 1,533,738 / 703,859
2010/11: 1,605,599 / 744,053
2011/12: 1,569,069 / 736,158
2012/13: 1,436,481 / 677,255
2013/14: 1,477,585 / 696,580
2014/15 (year to date): 731,574 / 345,789

Source: Gov.uk, December 2014 (year to date - September), Department for Transport

prefer the convenience of their own car or taxi services like Uber.

Similarly, EVs from the likes of Tesla and BMW i will remain niche lifestyle accessories for the rich due to their expense, charging hassle and flat battery concerns. City authorities will create some demand for EVs by prioritising them, from insisting new taxis are EVs to exemption from congestion charges. And as EVs are increasingly criticised for reasons such as the emissions created by electricity production, even the eco credentials that are their biggest selling point are under threat. Cars with increasingly clean and efficient petrol or diesel engines will rule the roads for decades to come.

What will happen

Two developments that will have an impact are driverless taxis and mobility apps for smartphones. Google has attracted a lot of attention with its self-driving car, but many other companies are just as advanced in their testing, with many of the latest road models already offering autonomous features such as adaptive cruise control and lane changing. While there are technical and legislative barriers to overcome, fully driverless cars are likely to be on the road in the next ten to 15 years. Initially they will be expensive to own; more immediately, driverless taxis may be cheaper than minicabs, and more comfortable and sociable as seats can face each other, with no need for a driver's seat.

Seamlessly jumping between different modes of transport has long been the stuff of transport visions. While piecemeal progress has been made through initiatives such as London Oyster Card, physically joining the dots between cars, trains, buses and planes requires more serious investment. The next wave of this innovation will happen on our phones. Apps like Citymapper, Uber and Hailo are already must-haves for urbanistas, and Helsinki has announced that it plans to roll out a 'mobility of demand' system by 2025, which will let Finns plan and pay for fully integrated journeys on their phone.

The system will knit everything from driverless cars and mini buses to shared bikes and ferries into a 'mesh of mobility'.

What could happen

To tackle congestion in cities like London, we need to not just make more use of existing roads by, for example, pruning back the number of bus lanes and allowing all types of taxis to use the ones that remain. More critically, we must invest in underground motorways, ring roads and car parks. How about an outer circle tube line too – oh, and a new airport?

Generally, however, innovation in transport will move forward in areas governed by the private sector. Vehicles will continue to become more connected, through added Wi-Fi on planes, trains and automobile. They will become more and more automated, as in driverless cars and trains. And we will increasingly manage our journeys through our smartphones – whether that's planning and paying for transport options, or controlling our own vehicles, such as the new Tesla cars, which allow owners to locate, warm up, unlock and start the car from their phones.

It's certainly progress. But for generations that have grown up in the supersonic age and beyond, it can all sound positively pedestrian.

Kevin McCullagh, Founder of Plan, a product strategy consultancy in London. Also writes, speaks and curates conferences on design, business and society.

23 November 2014

⇨ The above information is reprinted with kind permission from *The Telegraph*. Please visit www.telegraph.co.uk for further information.

Are solar panel road surfaces the path to the future?

How one company is hoping to lead the way by adapting solar panel technology to create a new road surface.

By Ucilia Wang

Imagine driving your car out of the garage and what you see is not the usual dark grey asphalt but a street of blue-green hexagonal tiles, with lane markings and traffic signs lit up by embedded LED bulbs.

The image might seem surreal, but a couple in Idaho is working on making it a reality. Meet Julie and Scott Brusaw, who eight years ago started a project to build a roadway embedded with solar cells. Several private and public grants later, the Brusaws are now in the middle of a fundraising campaign via Indiegogo to raise money to hire engineers, improve the design and bring Solar Roadways to the marketplace.

The campaign has fascinated the public and is closing in on $2 million, after surpassing the initial goal of $1 million. 'We need to tweak the design and look for a better way to manufacture them,' said Scott Brusaw. 'We've made the panels by hand.'

'Imagine driving your car out of the garage and what you see is not the usual dark grey asphalt but a street of blue-green hexagonal tiles'

Solar Roadways, the Brusaws' project, is certainly bold. They are not just proposing to build glass-topped solar panels that are rugged enough to withstand big trucks and heavy traffic and generate electricity for sale; they also envisage charging electric cars, perhaps wirelessly while the cars zoom down the highway. They are putting LED in the panels not only for marking roads but also for displaying advertising, at least for parking lot projects for businesses.

They're even looking at funnelling melted snow from the solar panels into an underground storage tank before sending it to a water treatment centre. Snow removal is critical to ensure the solar panels get sun, so the solar panels will be heated to melt the snow. But the melted water could refreeze and push up the panels if it's allowed to pool off the edge of the solar road, so funnelling is an option.

Note that all these proposed uses of a solar roadway are also ways for such a project to generate revenues. Figuring out ways to make a solar roadway project economically feasible will be a huge challenge, says Gregory Wilson, director of the National Center for Photovoltaics at the National Renewable Energy Laboratory, which is part of the US Department of Energy.

While the Brusaws are using some proven technologies, such as silicon solar cells and LED lighting, they need to design them to work well together and under weather and road conditions that pose different challenges to conventional solar panel installation (on a rooftop or in the field) or LED traffic signals and street lighting.

A novel technology often costs more, at least initially, until it's made in enough volume to reduce manufacturing expenses. Its price should also come down when there is enough demand to help recoup the initial research and development cost.

'A novel technology often costs more, at least initially, until it's made in enough volume to reduce manufacturing expenses'

Then there is the expense of maintaining a solar roadway. It will require monitoring to make sure each panel is producing the expected amount of solar electricity. Repairing or replacing the components, if not each panel, will have to be easy to minimise the extent of roadway closures.

Keeping a solar roadway clear of dirt and debris and out of shade, all of which lower electricity generation, will also be crucial in making the project financially attractive, Wilson said. The Solar Roadway project is attempting to address many of these operational and maintenance issues.

While a solar roadway doesn't have to cost the same as concrete or asphalt, it has to generate enough revenue or other benefits to justify its cost. 'I would love to see this project being economically viable,' said Wilson. 'It'll likely to be too expensive to be deployed everywhere. But it will have niche applications.'

Just how expensive paving a mile with Brusaws' solar panels will cost is a big unknown. The company has yet to finalise its design, which will dictate the types of materials used and the cost of buying and assembling them into panels.

Scott Brusaw declined to discuss potential costs and said he will have a better idea about the manufacturing cost after he wraps up the prototype design, funded by the US Highway Administration, next month.

The federal agency has given two grants, totalling $850,000, to the project.

The federal grants have made it possible for the Brusaws to show what they have come up with so far by paving a 12ft by 36ft space on their property with LED-embedded solar panels. The couple changed the shape of the panel from 12ft by 12ft square during the initial design to a hexagon. An assembly of hexagons, which collectively resemble the shape of a honeycomb, adds strength to the overall structure and also makes it easier for building curved roadways, Scott said.

Brusaw, who is an electrical engineer, wants to hire civil and structural engineers to help him to finalise the solar panel design. The current design uses two pieces of half-inch thick tempered glass to sandwich the solar cells, LED and other electronic components. Lab analyses show that a roadway using the current prototype can already handle 250,000lb, Brusaw said.

The glass is textured to help reduce the extent of skidding when it's raining.

The Brusaws wants to start making and selling their rugged solar panels before the end of the year. The city of Sandpoint, where the couple live, is set to become the first customer by installing the solar panels at a visitor centre parking lot.

5 June 2014

⇨ The above information is reprinted with kind permission from *The Guardian*. Please visit www. theguardian.com for further information.

The future of travel: what will holidays look like in 2024?

Hotels on the Moon, hologram staff, danger-zone tourism… this is how our holidays will look in 2024, or so says a new report. But we've got our own ideas – and would like to hear yours, too.

What does the future hold for travel? Check-in by robot? Budget space flights? Virtual holidays? Flight comparison site Skyscanner is offering a glimpse of what the 2024 holiday experience could be like with its Future of Travel report. We've digested the findings and come up with a few ideas that we think would benefit the world of travel. But what would you like to see in future? Give us your ideas in the comments below.

Space travel

They say: For the ultimate in 'serious traveller bragging rights', how about a brief time spent floating weightlessly in low Earth orbit? It's something that should become relatively affordable (i.e. $75,000) compared to the cost of, say, an actual Apollo-style excursion to the moon. That said, architects Foster + Partners are currently involved in a project with the European Space Agency exploring ways they could build structures on the Moon with the help of 3D printers, so a lunar hotel could be on the horizon.

We say: It's bad enough having to listen to someone recounting the time they befriended a local harem pants salesman during their gap year in India, let alone the time they accidentally sneezed in their own face while experiencing zero gravity. A moon colony, however, does pique our interest.

In a nutshell: Get saving.

Underwater experiences

They say: Sub-aquatic hotels will be a 'far more mainstream proposition' by 2024 and underwater tourism will certainly trump space travel. As Skyscanner CEO Gareth William says: 'I suspect you would get more from it, because there is more to see down there than in space.' That said, the Poseidon Underwater Resort in Fiji, which was due to open in 2008, is still nowhere near ready.

We say: It may not cost as much as space but sleeping with the fishes is still going to be beyond the budget of 99% of holidaymakers – when it does finally open, a week at the Poseidon resort in Fiji will cost £9,000.

In a nutshell: Don't hold your breath.

Local travel

They say: Peer-to-peer collaboration will take over the world, and within the next decade between five to 10% of people could be renting out their homes to travellers. Increasingly, ''social travel' – from accommodation to supper clubs and other experiences – will become part of the traditional travel industry. New tools will lead to collaboration between tourists and people in the destinations, helping create more localised and personal travel.

We say: As personal, authentic experiences go mainstream, what next for the current set of supper-clubbing, airbnbing globetrotters who like to think of themselves as travellers not tourists? The only way they will be able to distance themselves from the travelling masses muscling in on their territory is to drop the idea of social travel altogether (so 2014) and instead adopt an anti-social approach: the countryside will be awash with hipsters being mindful – alone – in the woods.

In a nutshell: Forget secret supper clubs – expect secret holidays.

Extreme travel

They say: In the further pursuit of 'bragging rights', tourists will start pursuing adventures in extreme destinations. Travellers will want to be the first to drop in on so-called 'forbidden zones', destinations once rendered inaccessible by conflict or political instability or, conversely, be among the last people to see a habitat or species threatened with extinction. Lebanon will become the new Dubai, Angola could take off too, and the chance to spot a bare-faced tamarin before the species dies out will be a lifetime holiday highlight for a lucky few.

We say: Firstly, anyone who goes on holiday for 'bragging rights' is an idiot. As for travelling to forbidden zones, fine if you've got a genuine interest – but even then let the story of Matthew Miller, the American who wanted to secretly investigate the human rights situation in North Korean prisons – and is now experiencing them at first hand – be a cautionary tale.

In a nutshell: Don't do it.

Five things we'd like to see in 2024

Airships, the return of

Ever since the Hindenberg disaster, the idea of travelling beneath a huge balloon of highly inflammable gas has – perhaps understandably – been on the back burner. But now they are back in development: safe, environmentally friendly and with the potential to stay in the air for weeks at a time, dirigible transportation seems to us like the closest we'll come to living in the clouds.

Transatlantic trains

London King's Cross to New York's Grand Central without changing trains? Someone needs to start digging that tunnel.

Virtual reality destination testing

In the future, holidays from hell should become inconceivable. One way of ensuring this is through virtual reality destination testing. Simply pop on an Oculus Rift headset and go for a stroll. Mould in the hotel room? Building work in the pool? Then go somewhere else or sort out the problem before you go. Never again shall unsuspecting holidaymakers be faced with such imperfections on arrival.

Multi-lingual brain implants

'Me… Want… Beer?' In the future, the linguistic ineptitude of British travellers will be an irrelevance thanks to the invention of multilingual brain implants that you can inject into your skull at all good chemists. The result will be perfect fluency in every language of the world, meaning you can buy souvenirs, argue with taxi drivers and, yes, order a beer, wherever you go.

Insta-hols brain zaps

(Probably) using the same technology of multilingual brain implants, in the future you won't even need to go on holiday to get that refreshed and relaxed feeling. Instead, just zap yourself with a 'holi-rod' and to be transported to your destination of choice. Two minutes later you'll be back in the office, this time with a brain full of wonderful memories, such as the delicious cocktails you drank in that underwater hotel, and how clean you feel from the intelligent shower you had that morning. Mega bragging rights indeed.

29 September 2014

⇨ The above information is reprinted with kind permission from *The Guardian*. Please visit www.theguardian.com for further information.

Transport innovation is not all about new technology

By Claire Haigh, Chief Executive of Greener Journeys

Successful innovation in transport doesn't need a revolutionary new technology. You don't need a greener vehicle or a clever integration that makes a transport system more efficient.

An effective policy or eye-catching campaign that convinces people to change their travel choices can work just as well. When it does, it is important that we sing the praises of such a success and learn our lessons.

One example is the older person's bus pass. Since they were introduced in 2006, bus passes have been extremely popular. 95% of bus users strongly support the policy, according to Passenger Focus figures, and last year more than 1.2 billion journeys were made by holders.

Of course, free bus passes help older people and people with disabilities lead more active lives. But there's another test. Does the policy represent good value for the taxpayer?

Greener Journeys, working with KPMG, recently undertook research that found that every £1 spent on the bus pass generates at least £2.87 in benefits to its users, other road users and the wider economy. That adds up to high value for money, according to Department for Transport guidance.

The benefits we found are extraordinarily wide-ranging. The bus pass allows older people to continue to volunteer, a sector which relies on them heavily to survive. It means they are more physically and mentally active, with knock-on benefits for healthcare. It benefits all road users through improved bus services, road decongestion and cuts to CO_2 emissions.

The list goes on and on. If the bus pass were taken away, our conclusion was that it would cost UK plc significantly in excess of £1.7 billion in economic benefits a year. All this shows that we must keep the bus pass and ensure that it's funded adequately in the years to come, especially as the population gets older.

But there's a bigger lesson here. The interconnections within our society and economy are incredibly deep, broad and complex, with the consequences and impacts of adding or removing something not always readily apparent.

Making sure we consider in detail why a policy or proposal is of wider socio-economic significance is a vital component in safeguarding it.

The analysis also plainly shows the wide impacts that empowering people to make a more sustainable transport choice can have on economy and society. We must make sure we shout about these, as although they may be obvious to us, it's clear they are not always to others.

13 October 2014

⇨ The above information is reprinted with kind permission from *Govtoday*. Please visit www.govtoday.co.uk for further information.

Key facts

⇨ In 2013, on average each person made 923 trips per year, compared with 1,094 in 1995/97 – a fall of 16%. (page 1)

⇨ The average distance travelled per person per year was 6% lower in 2013 than in 1995/97 – 6,983 miles compared with 6,584 miles. (page 1)

⇨ In 2013, 89% of all trips were by private transport modes. Trips by private transport modes have decreased by 18% since 1995/97. (page 1)

⇨ In 2013, the most common trip purpose was shopping, which accounted for 20% of all trips, followed by personal business and other escort trips with 19% of all trips. The least common trip purposes were for education (12% of all trips) and business (3% of all trips). (page 1)

⇨ As of 2 July 2014 the UK had the eighth highest petrol price in the 28-member EU. (page 3)

⇨ There are 35.2 million licensed vehicles in Great Britain including: 29.3 million cars (of which 9,412 are electric), 3.4 million vans and 465,860 lorries. (page 4)

⇨ 31% of households have two or more cars or vans. 44% of households have one car or van. 25% of households have no car or van. (page 4)

⇨ Transport is the second highest category of household spending after rent, fuel and power for the home, at £64.10 a week. (page 4)

⇨ Around 800,000 car-owning households spent at least 31% of their disposable incomes on buying and running a vehicle in 2012. (page 5)

⇨ According to ONS figures, the worst effects of commuting on personal well-being were associated with journey times of between 61 and 90 minutes. (page 6)

⇨ New research carried out by Campaign for Better Transport shows that since 2010, local authority funding for bus services has been slashed by 15 per cent (£44 million) with more than 2,000 routes being reduced or withdrawn entirely. (page 7)

⇨ On an average weekday 34,000 passengers use high-speed services. (page 11)

⇨ Road traffic injuries are the eighth leading cause of death globally, and the leading cause of death for young people aged 15–29. (page 13)

⇨ More than 80% of child road casualties occur on 30mph limited streets. (page 15)

⇨ According to Flightglobal's report, 2014's global fatal accident rate of one per 2.38 million flights makes 2014 the safest year ever for flying. (page 17)

⇨ Some 655,000 people work in the cycling economy – which includes bicycle production, tourism, retail, infrastructure and services – compared to 615,000 people in mining and quarrying, and just 350,000 workers directly employed in the steel sector. (page 18)

⇨ Walking or cycling to work is better for people's mental health than driving to work, according to new research by health economists at the University of East Anglia and the Centre for Diet and Activity Research (CEDAR). (page 20)

⇨ More than 25 million kilometres of new roads will be built worldwide by 2050. (page 22)

⇨ Compared to petrol cars, diesels produce 22 times the amount of particulate matter – a cause of cancer linked with the premature deaths of thousands of Britons each year. (page 23)

⇨ 'Around 30% of Scottish car club members decreased their annual mileage by an average of 3,546 miles, while 22% increased it by on average of just 1,051 miles' (Research by Carplus). (page 26)

⇨ As of October 2014, there are approximately 7,300 electric charging points across the UK. (page 27)

⇨ Four in ten under-40s would be interested in having a driverless car, though British people tend to think they won't catch on. (page 31)

Car club/car sharing

A car share organisation which allows customers to use vehicles as and when they require them, without bearing the cost of buying and running a car of their own. This is an economical and environmentally-friendly way to gain regular access to a car. Customers must cover their own fuel charges and will also be asked to pay a membership fee, allowing them access to one of the club's fleet of vehicles when required. Car clubs are becoming increasingly popular among commuters, especially in urban areas.

Commute

A journey between work and home made on a regular basis. Someone who regularly travels a set distance to their place of work is known as a commuter.

Congestion

When a large number of vehicles build up on any one stretch of road, causing very slow-moving or stationary traffic, the road is said to be congested. As most people in the UK now own and drive vehicles, congestion is becoming increasingly problematic.

The Congestion Charge

The Congestion Charge is a toll which motorists are required to pay in order to drive within the central London Congestion Charge Zone (CCZ). The controversial fee was introduced in 2003 with the aim of reducing congestion in the city centre. Cameras register the number plate of each vehicle as it enters the CCZ, and fines are imposed if the charge is not paid. There are some exemptions from the charge. It has been reported that due to the 'C-charge' (as it is known), traffic levels in the zone have dropped by around 20%

Driverless car

Also known as an autonomous car, self-driving car or robotic car. This type of vehicle is able to move without the input of humans and can drive 'all by itself'. These cars use techniques such as radar, CPS and computer vision to help sense their surroundings. Some driverless cars have the ability to allow humans to override it if they want to, whereas others have zero input from humans (e.g. no steering wheel or pedals). There is much debate about the ethics of autonomous cars: for example, should a robot be in complete control of safety decisions (are they 'human' enough to make the right choice?)? Should humans be allowed to override driverless cars (some argue that human interference actually causes accidents rather than the technology itself)?

Electric car

This type of vehicle is fuelled by electricity, which can be recharged at specially-designed charging points. Electric vehicles are considered a green alternative to petrol- or diesel-engine cars, as they have no tail pipe emissions and are therefore less damaging to the environment. A 2008 study by the Department for Business Enterprise and Regulatory Reform predicted that electric vehicles could cut carbon dioxide and greenhouse gas emissions by at least 40%. Electric vehicles are still an emerging technology, but they are expected to have a big impact on the future of automobile production.

Emissions

Emissions are the exhaust fumes that are released from vehicles as they burn fuel. They are damaging to both the environment and people's health, containing, among other chemicals and greenhouse gases, carbon dioxide and carbon monoxide.

High-speed rail

High-speed rail is a relatively new form of transport: a passenger rail service that is able to travel at much greater speeds than traditional trains. High-speed trains travel via direct routes at speeds of around 120–160 miles per hour.

Private transport

Private modes of transport is something that is personal such as walking, bicycle, car, motorcycle, private hire buses, minibus, motorcaravan and dormobile.

Public transport

Where the public shares a mode of transport, such as buses, surface rail, underground, ferries and domestic airplanes.

Road safety

Road traffic injuries are the eighth leading cause of death globally, and the leading cause of death for young people aged 15–29. More than a million people die each year on the world's roads, and the cost of dealing with the consequences of these road traffic crashes runs to billions of dollars. Current trends suggest that by 2030 road traffic deaths will become the fifth leading cause of death unless urgent action is taken.

Road tax

A tax that all road users are required to pay in order to own and run a vehicle. It is against the law to drive an untaxed vehicle on the road. The amount of tax levied is based on the size and type of the vehicle. Modern 'road tax' – Vehicle Excise Duty – goes into general taxation.

Transport poverty

Transport poverty refers to the ability of a household to afford running a car; the rising cost of running a car has started to place a significant strain on people's budgets. Around 800,000 car-owning households spent at least 31% of their disposable incomes on buying and running a vehicle in 2012.

Assignments

Brainstorming

⇨ In small groups, discuss what you know about transport. Consider the following questions:

- What is transport?

- How many different modes of transport can you list?

- What is the different between private and public transport (list some examples)?

- What do you think the transport of the future will be like?

Research

⇨ Using online newspaper archives do some research into electric cars and their role in the future of transport. In particular, look for articles which cover the debate over the viability of developing electric cars as the 'next big thing'. Write a report on your findings.

⇨ Carry out a research project into transport in your area. First of all, make a list of all the modes of transport that are available to your local community. Then conduct a survey among community members to establish which methods are the most popular. You could also contact influential community members for more information on the transport situation: a local councillor, for example. Summarise your findings in a report.

⇨ Compile a detailed report about driverless cars. What are the arguments for and against driverless cars? Who would benefit from driverless cars? Who would lose out?

⇨ Imagine you work for a charity that promotes road safety. Plan a social media marketing campaign that will raise awareness of road traffic injuries and how to improve national road safety.

⇨ Research the Cycle to Work scheme. Do you think this is a good idea? Does it encourage people to take up cycling? Based on this idea, try and come up with your own scheme to help encourage people to cycle more.

Design

⇨ Ideas for a new modes of transport designed to ease congestion are constantly being sought. In groups of four, brainstorm the problems and challenges associated with current modes of transport: for example, road congestion and rail prices. Based on the issues that you have identified, devise a new mode of transport to help address one of these issues. Draw a diagram of your invention and provide details on how expensive it would be to run, whether it would be suited to city transport or long distances and any associated environmental benefits.

⇨ Imagine that a new guided busway has been built in your local town. Create an eye-catching poster advertising the service, encouraging people to use the busway instead of driving.

⇨ Design a poster that promotes car sharing. Try to think of some unique ways to encourage people to car share.

Oral

⇨ As a class, read and discuss *Air travel is safe and getting safer – whatever else you might have read* (page 17).

⇨ Read the article *Public Health professionals call for 20mph limits* on page 15 and discuss the author's point of view. Consider other point of views, such as residents who live in the area or people who commute through that area.

⇨ As a group discuss how methods of travel have changed over time. What was travel like in the past? How does it compare to now? What will travel be like in the future?

Reading/writing

⇨ The articles *Five years on and high-speed rail has 'transformed the economic fortunes of Ashford'* (page 9) and *The case against High Speed 2 (HS2)* (page 12). Consider the benefits and drawbacks of the high-speed rail system in Britain. Summarise each argument, for and against, in two short paragraphs. Which do you agree with?

⇨ Watch *I, Robot* (rated 12A) and write a review exploring how the director deals with the theme of transport (specifically driverless cars).

⇨ Write a diary entry from the perspective of a person with a disability using transport (e.g. blind or uses a wheelchair). Consider how this disability could impact on your travel experience on different modes of transport. Do you have to make plans in advance? Do they have adequate facilities?

⇨ What is meant by the term 'transport poverty'? Write an essay which explains what transport poverty means and how we as a society can help to tackle this issue. You might find *Transport poverty 2014* on page 5 helpful.

Acknowledgements

The publisher is grateful for permission to reproduce the material in this book. While every care has been taken to trace and acknowledge copyright, the publisher tenders its apology for any accidental infringement or where copyright has proved untraceable. The publisher would be pleased to come to a suitable arrangement in any such case with the rightful owner.

Images

All images courtesy of iStock, except cover and page iii © Dorothy Hübner, page 20 © Jackie Staines and page 27 © The U.S Army.

Icons on pages 19, 21 and 38 are reproduced courtesy of Freepik.

Illustrations

Don Hatcher: pages 16 & 28. Simon Kneebone: pages 22 & 35. Angelo Madrid: pages 44 & 36.

Additional acknowledgements

Editorial on behalf of Independence Educational Publishers by Cara Acred.

With thanks to the Independence team: Mary Chapman, Sandra Dennis, Christina Hughes, Jackie Staines and Jan Sunderland.

Cara Acred

Cambridge

May 2015